Bitches and Abdicators

TONI SCALIA

Bitches and Abdicators

M. EVANS AND COMPANY, INC.
New York

Library of Congress Cataloging in Publication Data

Scalia, Toni.
  Bitches and abdicators.

    1. Women—Psychology. 2. Control (Psychology)
3. Assertiveness (Psychology) I. Title.
HQ1206.S34   1985   305.4'2   85-1636

ISBN 0-87131-455-X

M. Evans and Company, Inc.
216 East 49 Street
New York, New York 10017

Design by Lauren Dong

Manufactured in the United States of America

9 8 7 6 5 4 3 2

To my sons, Jason and Russell Scalia,
and my mother,
Jean Martone Daniels

.

Contents

Acknowledgments

I want to express my appreciation to Grace Kennedy for her invaluable help in preparing and initially editing the manuscript; to Evan Marshall, my literary agent at The Sterling Lord Agency, for his excellent assistance, support, and enthusiasm; to all the people at M. Evans, specifically Linda Cabasin, Diane Gedymin, and Herb Katz; and finally to all those women who shared their experiences with me.

Chapter One

Bitches and Abdicators

I have written this book for every woman who has had to force herself to move away from a relationship that did not satisfy her needs and wants; for every woman too afraid to fully exercise her authority as a parent; for every woman who has been worked over in the world of business. I have written it as well for every woman juggling a career and a lover, enjoying the appurtenances of a new image, free to come and go as she chooses—and yet feeling a nagging lack of satisfaction. My message to all of them is clear: You can relinquish control or you can take control. In my terms, you can be *abdicator* or you can be *bitch*. The choice is yours.

These terms seem harsh. They are. They did not come as the result of an intellectual exercise. They came from personal experience—my own, and the experiences of the many women I interviewed. And both terms are much more than an attempt to categorize behavior. They not only describe what we do but how we are perceived either consciously or subconsciously by others. The sad truth is that most men, even now, are more comfortable with abdicator behavior from women. The woman who deliberately challenges and provokes is still called a bitch. So, why not turn the term around? If to be a bitch means that a decent and fair person suddenly expresses her own needs and wants, then being a bitch is surely a goal worth seeking. Of course, it makes for certain problems. If *bitch* is now a positive term, what do we do with the old-fashioned Bette Davis kind of bitch? Do we call her the bad bitch as opposed to the good one I advocate? Perhaps, or perhaps we should just forget altogether the bad bitch for now. This book is only about the good one. And still there are problems. What about the times when the good bitch must abdicate selectively? Are there such times? Of course there are, and we shall deal with them. There are always paradoxes. But even with the paradoxes, the choices and the options are very clear. This book is intended as a blueprint: a plan for change any woman can follow.

From my personal experience, I learned that the ability to create alternatives and take advantage of options was much more under my control than I had either been led to or allowed myself to believe. And this was reinforced by the stories of the women who shared their experiences with me. What I found was that women who relinquished control did so as a result of certain patterns I call *abdicator behaviors*. When we abdicate, we do the following:

- We avoid confrontation.
- We complain to our friends about our lovers' behavior and vent our anger only where it's safe.
- We play nice guy at work and deny the realities of political power.
- We don't claim ownership of the money we make and keep ourselves financially immature.

As I began my own attempt to move from acquiescence to equality, a healthy anger—directed at myself for acquiescing and at others for insisting and expecting me to—replaced complacency. And self-pity was replaced by an unforgiving honesty. And again both my experience and my research demonstrated that acting out a changed response to the social restraints placed on women (and their acceptance of those restraints) results in the changed response being viewed as a *personal* aberration.

What happens is that when just anger replaces complacency and when honesty replaces self-pity, the personal behavior that results is *challenged* before it can become challenging to the issue that made the behavioral change necessary. And the woman opting for this change is called bitch.

We no longer exhibit *weakness*—we demonstrate *strength* —and are called bitch.

We no longer comply—we insist on authority—and are called bitch.

I am not using the term *bitch* in the pejorative sense. I am using it to reflect the cultural label that is applied to women who, as they practice self-determination, behave in ways that are contrary to the behavior that is expected of them by their husbands and lovers, children and families, bosses and subordinates. Almost without fail, when a woman steps out of the role society has assigned to her, she is called bitch.

Since this is our cultural reality, I have redefined the term so that it carries a positive meaning.

BITCH: An aggressive woman who stands her ground and speaks her piece; one who operates on a quid pro quo basis and who behaves in such a way as to receive in equal measure the love, nurturing, comfort, and understanding that she supplies in her love relationships and parenting; a woman who does not rationalize either her successes or failures in the work place and aggressively pursues her individual potential.

This definition and the following one of *abdicator* were borne out by my many interviews with women:

ABDICATOR: A woman who surrenders and relinquishes her adult authority and personal dignity in areas over which she is both capable and deserving of control;

one who, by her behavior, travels the pathway of self-denial.

Throughout the research and the writing of this book I have focused on behaviors: behaviors that either prevent women from enjoying or allow them to enjoy satisfactory love relationships; behaviors that either prevent women from becoming adequate parents or allow them to exercise mature and nurturing parental judgment; behaviors that either render women impotent within their work affiliations or aid them in utilizing their talents and intelligence to further their careers and professions.

Those actions that inhibit us from developing our potential, prevent us from satisfying our needs, and allow others to determine and define who we are, what we are capable of, and what we should do, I have labeled *abdicator behaviors*. Those actions that permit us to grow, allow us to pursue aggressively the satisfaction of our needs, and let us determine for ourselves who we are and what we want to be, I have labeled *bitch behaviors*.

There are significant contrasts between these two behavioral categories:

- The abdicator acquires; the bitch earns.
- The abdicator avoids; the bitch confronts.
- The abdicator is halted in her development; the bitch grows.
- The abdicator is reactive; the bitch initiates action.
- The abdicator hides her discontent, thus relinquishing her needs; the bitch keeps her discontent in focus and gives voice to her needs.

Certainly, I have drawn these categories along strongly polarized lines, and I have done so in order to make vivid the contrast between the two. There is a point, however, where the setting up of such stark contrasts can be misleading. And that point occurs in the link between abdication and trust.

There are situations where *selective abdication*—abdication by choice—is a healthy and necessary expression of trust. Selective abdication occurs when we have honestly assessed our skills and abilities and make a thoughtful decision to turn over a task to someone we judge more capable than ourselves. And we do that in work and in parenting.

Selective abdication—again the healthy kind—occurs when after honest and thoughtful assessment of our love partner's behavior toward us, we turn over part of ourselves to be cared for, to be nurtured, to be loved. We give our trust. However, most forms of abdication are nonselective—that is, we abdicate in response to someone's else's wishes, not in response to our own. Such abdication is a form of self-betrayal. This betrayal, in turn, results in mistrust of self. Having withheld trust from ourselves, it can only be falsely given, half-heartedly given, or angrily given to others. Only by recognizing and understanding our abdicating behaviors can we begin the process of trusting ourselves. Only by practicing bitch behaviors can we willingly give trust to others.

I wish I could say that, having stumbled my way through these changes, I decided to use my formal training to research and write up the process. I hold a bachelor's degree in psychology from New York University and a master's in sociology from Washington University, where I am now completing my doctorate. I wish I could say that, but that's not the way it happened. It happened because of a corporate reorganization, a change in company direction, my own classically scripted and very well-acted abdicator behavior—and the job loss that followed.

I have no idea whether the decision to write this book is indicative of healthy self-confidence or supreme arrogance. And I don't care. The point is that I did it.

Like many women in the work force, I have often been in the position of "being the only one." I was the only female faculty member in the Department of Administration of Justice of a midwestern university system; I was the only female associate director in an international training and development consulting firm headquartered in the Midwest. My position there required that I travel around the country and conduct management development seminars for several Fortune 500 firms. Participants in the seminars spanned organizational levels from chief executive officer to entry-level managerial and supervisory personnel. The seminars focused on behavioral solutions to problems encountered on the job. It took only two or three seminars to recognize that the problems encountered by women were far different from those experienced by men. Not only were the problems different, but the behavioral solutions that men and women were using to resolve them differed as well. In an effort to be as accurate as I could be in both my analysis and in the solutions I was offering, I began to keep a journal describing and detailing these differences. Where the men practiced either accommodating behaviors or "true grit" leadership roles, the women either gave in and abdicated or gave up their sainthood and assumed bitch roles. The journal that I kept became part of the research that I later incorporated.

When I was later hired as a training manager for a large retail chain operation, my role as counselor for solving on-the-job interpersonal problems provided me with additional and valuable material. After leaving the retail firm, I spent a year gathering additional data and formalizing my research. I then began to write full time. I renewed contacts I had made in past work efforts and held individual interviews and group discussions with women from New York to San Francisco. I collected responses from well over 250 women, which are herein recounted.

It was during my last year of research that another crucial difference between abdicating and bitch behaviors surfaced. It was quite apparent that those women who displayed abdicating behaviors at work were far less able to make a distinction between their corporate behavior and personal behavior than were their more aggressive sisters. This led me to expand the research to include a description and analysis of abdicating and bitch behaviors within the two primary areas of personal life: love relationships and parenting.

Here again the contrasts and distinctions between abdicating and bitch behaviors were significant. These are some of the contrasts I found within the love relationship:

- The bitch initiates behavior in the face of fear and anxiety; the abdicator maintains the status quo through compliance and with depression.
- The bitch assumes personal responsibility for her well-being; the abdicator relies on others.
- The bitch seeks her own activities; the abdicator lives vicariously through the actions of others.
- The bitch creates choices and chooses; the abdicator does not think in terms of options or alternatives.
- The bitch tunes in to her subjective feelings, using them to filter her surroundings; the abdicator rationalizes her discontent in terms of "they," "it," and "society."
- The bitch views her mate as an individual who wishes support, as she does, who needs to be cared for, as she does, and who seeks a balance between freedom and responsibility, as she does. The abdicator views her mate as caretaker.
- The bitch relies on her authority as an adult; the abdicator asks permission as a child.

The bottom line is that the abdicators maintained unions that did not fulfill their needs, whereas those women practicing bitch behaviors either gained equality within their existing relationships or moved on to another that met their needs, wants, and desires.

Not surprisingly, many of the women carried their behaviors over into the realm of parenting. The abdicator is revealed as a mother in name only, as she gives over her responsibility for child rearing to husband, lover, family, friends, and institutions. She exhibits reactive rather than proactive responses, and passive and easy-way-out actions such as bribing and guilt offerings. She compromises and behaves inconsistently with respect to the goals she has for her children and the behavior she expects of them. Ultimately, she offers her children limited need fulfillment and conditional affection.

The bitch as mother is revealed as a winning parent as opposed to a whining one. She offers unconditional love but conditional behavioral choices for her children, based on her assessment of both social values and the child's potential. She maintains a declarative, imperative "I'm the parent here" attitude, with the goals she has for her children serving as the sieve through which she filters their behavior.

In love relationships, role differences, homebody versus breadwinner activities, and the assumed and actual cultural differences between men and women can hide the distinctions between abdicator and bitch behaviors. In my individual interviews and group discussions, it was difficult and it took much time and effort to draw out these behaviors and to truly understand the consequences.

In parenting, there is the given that since you bear the title of parent you must be in control. Or that the incident being discussed represents "only a phase" that the child was in. Here again, the behaviors and consequences were difficult to ferret out in many of the histories and cases I researched.

This was not true in the work place. Here I could see woman versus woman, abdicator versus bitch. Role differentiation did not come into play. Gender was so obviously no longer an issue. The battleground was the work place. The lines were clearly drawn and the distinctions were clear:

- The abdicator chooses security; the bitch chooses risk taking.
- The abdicator monitors her behavior, so she is not seen as "taking advantage of situations"; the bitch uses her environment without feeling the need to apologize.
- The abdicator maintains a tunnel vision approach to her work; the bitch searches for relationships, analyzes processes, and synthesizes contrasting approaches.
- The abdicator refuses to become political or denies the existence of politics; the bitch enters political realities,

sometimes with bravado and always with determination.

- The abdicator says "I can't be that way"; the bitch conditions herself to play the bastard.
- The abdicator maintains her idealism; the bitch chooses to renounce her sainthood, her misplaced idealism.
- The abdicator seeks justice through "by the book" compliance; the bitch seeks vengeance through excellence and success.
- The abdicator keeps bringing home her paycheck; the bitch often risks bringing in double or nothing.
- The abdicator chooses to make a living; the bitch chooses to make a life.

As abdicator and as bitch, woman is perpetrator. As long as she acts against herself, she is excused. But the bitch is put on trial.

Submissive and acquiescent behavior has been judged acceptable feminine behavior by women, men, and society and its laws. Control, authority, equality, and strength when exhibited by women have been and still are subject to personal and public censure. Challenge is the rule when women leave the realm of acquiescence and achieve control over the direction of their lives. And it is when they react to this challenge that women are put on trial.

My primary emphasis is on helping women successfully manage the challenge and effect behavioral change. Behavioral change does not occur if we sugarcoat the consequences of existing behaviors and soft-sell the need for new behaviors. To that end, I have used hard-hitting and forceful language that presents strong contrasts between abdicating and bitch behaviors.

When change is the objective, the kind approach is the candid approach. This book is nothing if not candid in both the presentation of the case histories and in the description of the impact that abdicator and bitch behaviors have on both the women who practice them and on the people—husbands, lovers, children, and work associates—whom they interact with.

There is no doubt that there are social obstacles to equality, strength, and authority for women. But—although they are different in both kind and degree—these obstacles exist for men as well. The big news is this: *There is a greater difference in the behavior each of the sexes uses to assume equality, demonstrate strength, and take authority than there is in either the kind or the degree of restraints that each is subjected to.*

This last will be hard to swallow, especially for those of us who have spent years playing the role of abdicator. But stay with me. I'm not assessing responsibility here. I'm assessing behavior.

Who Are the Abdicators?
Who Are the Bitches?

Are we abdicators or bitches by age, profession, income, education, experience, ability, or history? No!

Bitch and abdicator behaviors are different, and the quality of life that goes with each of them is sometimes as far apart as fulfillment and despair, but they share—these bitches and abdicators—very similar profiles.

The women who shared their experiences with me vary in age from twenty-six to seventy-two; some are married, some are divorced, some are single women. Some have successful marriages, some have remarried after divorce, others have taken a series of lovers in both monogamous and non-monogamous relationships. Some have borne children, others have adopted them, and others, either by choice or circumstance, have not been involved in parenting. All of them are in the work world; some define themselves as "only working because I have to make a living." Some define themselves as career oriented and have sought upward mobility. Many are recognized experts in their professions and others are in the process of becoming so. Their salaries range from \$12,000 to \$80,000, and the years spent in the work force vary from seven to thirty-six. They span the range from lower middle class to upper middle class, and their educational experiences range from high school through graduate study. Their behaviors, whether as bitch or abdicator, do not represent the extremes of normal behavior. These women are not on the fringes of the well adjusted. They did not initiate relationships with bizarre men who devastated them physically or who exhibited behaviors beyond the range of normalcy. Their children are average or above-average individuals, none of whom have acted out in antisocial ways and all of whom have expressed the mischievousness, curiosity, and freedom testing common to childhood. Their work situations have been peopled by individuals who were not out of the ordinary either in the giving of their support or in the withholding of it.

These women share the social and psychological norms of the 1980s culture and have lived within them. Their uniqueness is the uniqueness that we all have by virtue of our individual experiences. They are your neighbors, friends, and acquaintances. They are your mothers, sisters, and daughters.

Both the bitch and the abdicator responses made by these women crossed the lines of age, education, profession, and experience, within their love relationships, in parenting, and within their work affiliations. Women in their thirties abdicated as much in their love relationships as did women in their fifties. Women with degrees in psychology and well read in the arts of child rearing relinquished as much control in parenting as did their less-informed sisters. Women who were recognized experts in their professions gave up as much control in their work situations as did the women who were just starting out.

That these behaviors crossed these lines and continue to persist in the face of the women's movement, the supposed increase in child-care activities by the male partner, and legislated rules for equality in business is both remarkable and shocking. It is shocking because those of us who were brought up in the fifties, grew up in the sixties, and stood up in the seventies believed that our daughters would stand up as they grew up. We thought we had paved the way. We thought our daughters could stand on our gains and go beyond them. But they haven't.

They may not get married. *But* they live together, and she works while he finishes school and he starts his climb up the corporate ladder.

They may continue with school. *But* she goes part-time and he attends full time.

They may not have children right away. *But* when they come, she plays the role of primary parent.

They may both work as career professionals. *But* she makes 69 cents for every dollar he makes, and he handles the family finances. And when a career move comes along for her, she takes it only if it does not uproot him.

We paid a high price for the gains we'd hoped our daughters would inherit. We dissolved our marriages. We reared our children as single parents. We started out in our thirties at the bottom of the work ladder after putting our husbands through in their twenties.

We did not expect that our daughters would, as we did, give up over a decade of their very precious lives before they would stand up and take control of their environment. But they did. And they will continue to do so—all those lovely generations to come—unless and until they can exorcise, through their behavior, their acceptance of pejorative cultural labels that prevent them from coming into their own.

Chapter Two

The Price of Abdicating

Relinquishing versus Taking Control

The menu of behavioral choices is a simple one to read, but making the right selection is far more difficult. Only when the behavioral ranges are understood, together with their consequences, gains, risks, and emotional highs and lows, can a valid choice be made. If the choice is not valid, our lives become happenstance and luck, based only on past abilities and experiences rather than on change.

It is the thesis of this book that the ability to take control over one's life situation is directly related to the behavior expressed. And further, barring the presence of clinically neurotic behaviors and actions, the ability to display self-determining control behaviors has very little to do with past events and experiences.

Women have been taught to deny themselves the physical pleasures that their bodies allow; and they have learned to overcome these teachings.

Women have been taught to be submissive to authority; and they have learned to overcome those teachings.

Women have been taught to feign weakness rather than demonstrate strength; and they have learned to overcome this as well.

We can learn to do away with any inhibitions or old wounds from the past. It is behavior that initiates the learning process. To effect change, all we need to do is force ourselves to act appropriately.

Behavior is, after all, interactional. It is the impact that our behavior has on another person that determines the responses and reactions we receive. We usually have no difficulty understanding the impact that we have on others with respect to how we dress or speak. We can certainly recognize the impact that we have on others by virtue of our position in the community or in the work place. Gaining equality within love or marital relationships, developing strength in parenting, and commanding authority within work situations require that we understand the impact our behavior has in the daily one-to-one interactions that occur in these areas.

We can come across as weak or strong, as in control or yielding. We can behave in ways that cause others to listen to us or ignore us. We can choose the way we want to be perceived and we can behave in ways that will match our choice. But only if we are aware of the behavioral options.

The concept that behavior can be learned certainly provides no earthshaking insight. Behaviorists have been demonstrating this for years. What is revealing is to review detailed accounts of the behavioral ranges, options, and alternatives that are available to us. Some of these options, such as rationalizations and refusing to question values, cause us to give up control and assume the role of abdicator. Other alternatives, such as confrontation and the use of any of the techniques that give us a realistic sense of self, aid us in self-determination and thus allow us to exercise control.

Practicing bitch behaviors helps us to create alternatives and to recognize choices. Abdicating behaviors strip us of the process of adapting and transforming our lives. One of the best examples I can give you of abdication in the love relationship is the woman who says to her husband, "If you're having an affair, don't tell me about it." While abdicating her right to that information, she also disallows the possibility of enjoying a similar sexual pleasure outside of her primary relationship.

Another illustration of abdication is when women find themselves single parents and deny themselves a sexual partner because it brings them into conflict with their image of mothering, even when ex-husbands don't deny themselves sex when the kids come to visit.

The best example from the work place is the now-familiar case of Geraldine Ferraro, who, in response to being attacked for not disclosing her husband's tax returns, said, "If you've ever been married to Italian men, you know what it's like." In identifying herself with a housewife stereotype, she abdicated her role as a leader.

The newest version of encouraging abdication is the "supportive" man, pushing "supportiveness" to the point where he is really taking control. This works when a man "advises" a woman about her career and always urges caution rather than aggressiveness. He tells her how to be "liked" by her colleagues rather than how to pay attention to the political realities.

Most women exhibit the behavior of both the abdicator and the bitch in all three areas: in the love relationship, in parenting, and in work associations. The movement from one to the other is a process of choosing, testing, and fine tuning as abdicator behaviors are exchanged for self-determining or bitch behaviors.

Many of us find ourselves wearing an abdicator hat with our mates and a bitch hat when mothering. At work we are either abdicator (and liked) or bitch (and distrusted). We wear these hats unconsciously. In order to opt for self-determination, we have to be prepared to choose the hat we wear consciously. For most women, this is a confusing move.

It's confusing because while we recognize that old behavior patterns aren't working, we still haven't gotten a firm hold on the new ones. And so we have a tendency to swing in pendulum fashion from old patterns to new ones and back again. We're not quite sure what it is we want, why we want it, or how to go about it. And all too often, as we'll see in the stories to come, we avoid discussing these changes with the people we interact with.

When our choice is a conscious one and represents a valid selection of options and alternatives, we create rules. They become apparent, and we can then choose either to follow them or ignore them. For some of us this process is hindered because we cannot accept the negative responses we receive as a result of the change in our behavior. If we are not behaviorally prepared to handle these responses, we begin to believe that we are behaving in an overly demanding and self-destructive manner as we attempt to gain control of our environment.

The abdicator is not prepared behaviorally to move from acquiescence to equality. Instead, she relies on behaviors that will give her peace at any price. Unfortunately the price is measured in both time and the quality of life: time spent in years of living in situations that do not meet her needs, wants, and desires; and a quality of life that is measured in terms of waiting for change instead of initiating it, nurturing ghosts instead of lovers, and spending life instead of living it.

The primary reason for the abdicator's inability to meet the negativism she encounters is that she is not able to transfer her skills and personal history, knowledge, intellect and wit, joy and hope from one area of her life to another. The inability to transfer experience from one area of our lives to another prevents us from initiating change and taking risks.

Abdicators are not risk takers. Bitches initiate change, take risks, and stand on the shoulders of their sense of self-history to build creatively more fulfilling lives.

For all of us there are areas in our lives where we have achieved a degree of success, made it through a difficult time, or accomplished more than we thought we could, areas within which we have taken actions that make us proud of ourselves. We saw that through; we didn't fall apart; we won that one. These are triumphs!

Abdicators do not transfer triumphs. Bitches revel in them.

Although the abdicator may keep a balance sheet between fulfillment and discontent, she keeps her tally *within* one area of her life rather than *among* all the areas of her life. If my work is going well, then I can put up with not having my needs met on the home front. If I am contented at home, then I need not concern myself with my business life. She breaks up her discontent, scattering and hiding its pieces here and there, with the result that she settles for less than what she wants and for less than what she is capable of. On a very pragmatic level, this thinking causes her to relinquish her financial responsibility and prevents her from preparing for crucial and unavoidable life changes. She does not prepare herself for a life after child rearing, she does not prepare herself for life accidents—the death of a loved one, a financial reversal, a personal illness, or the philosophical changes that come with age. Again, she *spends* her life rather than live it.

The bitch is a planner. Because she chooses to take control of her environment, she prepares herself, using the mental gymnastics necessary to seek alternatives, to understand what choices are available, and to create situations within which she can be comfortable. She is in the business of *making* a life.

I am going to introduce you first to women who abdicated in their love relationships. Some of them you will meet again because they have crossed the line and gone through the process of bitchhood. For many of the women that you will meet, my intrusion into their personal experiences with their husbands and lovers and with their successes and failures was painful. It called forth past actions and behaviors, the consequences of which they still lived with. It was also a gratifying experience—this sharing—because they were able to witness their own growth.

PART ONE

Love

Chapter Three

The Love Relationship

Abdicators in Love

Perhaps the most difficult area within which to move toward more self-determined behavior is within the love relationship. It is difficult because it is usually the first time that the woman has lived within a unit sanctioned by adulthood. We have been given permission to be adults because we have done something that adults do. We have entered a love union, and whether or not that union is legalized through marriage, it receives public sanction. That sanction, because of the adult status it confers on us, is something we do not want to lose, and the way we keep it is to compromise.

Society has relegated to the woman the role of primary compromiser. When she accepts that assignment, she begins the process of becoming an abdicator. The key word here is *primary*. Compromise becomes abdication when one person's work takes precedence over another's; when one person makes the financial decisions; when one person's friends serve as the mainstay of the couple's social activities. When

31

one person becomes the teller and the other becomes the listener, the art and the virtue of compromise turn into the thoughtless vice of abdication.

The woman who adopts the role of the abdicator within the love relationship leaves herself open to the following behavior from her lover or spouse:

"I would have discussed it with my wife, but I didn't want to (upset her, talk to her about it before it became definite, get her hopes up high, run the risk of her telling her mother, friends, and so on)."

These reactions directly imply that her mate is both discounting and invalidating her. He is indicating that he does not view her as a bona fide and responsible adult. His beliefs are that she cannot handle disappointments, cannot deal with unresolved situations, cannot cope with worry, and is unable to keep confidences. He has effectively prevented her from joining him as an equal partner in decision making that will have an impact on her life situation. *He has removed her discretionary authority*. But how does this loss of authority occur?

Evelyn's story provides one set of answers to this question. I first met Evelyn when she attended a seminar I conducted on affirmative action. At that time there was little of her behavior that would have typed her as an abdicator. At fifty-five years old she looked much younger than her years. She is petite, with flashing black eyes and a quick wit. Her energy comes across in her fast-paced conversation, her ability to pick up on new ideas, and the analytical way she has of getting to the bottom line. She has been in the work world for over thirty years and commands an income in the mid-twenties. Now divorced, after an eleven-year marriage, and well finished with child rearing—her son is twenty-seven—Evelyn is in the process of setting up a small business.

I interviewed Evelyn several times individually, and she took part in some of the group discussions as well. She is included here for two reasons. First, because her experience typifies that of so many of the women I interviewed, regardless of age, and second, because the abdicating behaviors she made use of in dealing with the realities she faced over a decade ago are being practiced full swing by women who could be her daughters.

The best starting point in Evelyn's story is the self-description she sent me in a cover letter that accompanied the résumé I had asked her for.

Dear Toni:

Enclosed is the résumé that you requested and here is an additional list of some of the things I've dipped into:

Hold a BA in piano performance, theory and organ from the _____ College of Music (now defunct); career originally was bent toward concert pianist—unfortunately, as my teacher moaned, I met (ugh) "Boys!"—but, actually, I discovered the world, wanted to write, travel, found an orphanage, be an architect, go into show business, etc. At age 12, was given choice of going the concert route or taking another—I chose another. Was an organist/choir director, here and there, for about 8 years. Still keep my hand (?) in through singing in professional-level choir.

While married, worked variously as a loan processor with a federal agency, assistant to the president-treasurer of a manufacturing company, but mostly assisted in family business—designed a four-family apartment which we subsequently built and I managed (at a profit), played secretary, office manager, drafter, purchaser, expediter, complaint manager, bookkeeper, wined and dined clients, and carried money to the bank, when I wasn't a substitute teacher in the elementary-junior high and high schools (English and business), teaching my class of private piano pupils, building a new house, bringing up son, playing Mrs. Mayor, shining the house, dodging and buffering husband's temper tantrums. Also member of library board (president 2 years plus other offices; instrumental on committee to establish county-wide library through State Library), Athenian Club (where I delivered literary papers and helped others with research, which gained me a reputation for being erudite—I wasn't, they hadn't heard it before), headed Heart Fund and other fund-raising drives, Community Betterment Association (formed and directed a chorus for annual performance), worked with Easter Seals and all those PTA and school functions. Was asked to run for school board (to serve as the "school house lawyer"—my husband wouldn't hear of it). Meanwhile, carried boats, floated the major streams in MO, camping out of a canoe for weeks at a time, dealt with vacation property in Ozarks, got shot at on sand bars, piloted us through temper tantrums held in deep water, and made a lot of discoveries along the way including how *not* to have a miscarriage and how NOT to get a divorce!

Back in _____, not in résumé, was charter member of the original Community Relations Council, served on _____ Alumni/Student committees, Bicentennial steering committee for 6-program series, "The Humanities in the City," various committees with Press Club; planned post-annual conference tour for WICI to historical sites in the East; served on Channel _____ advisory committees, etc., etc.

Have traveled to much of the U.S., western Europe, England, Egypt, Lebanon, Israel, Cuba (pre-Castro) and have an incurable wanderlust. There, you have it— what more can I say?

Evelyn

Evelyn's letter speaks eloquently both for her and about her. But the contrast between her letter and her behavior is enormous. In the world of work, from music to literary research and from fund raising to the family business, Evelyn exercised her intellectual abilities. But only to a point. With her tacit permission, her husband played the role of traffic cop, and Evelyn acquiesced. And because her "husband wouldn't hear of it," she declined an offer to run for the school board, received no remuneration for her contribution to the family business, and effectively joined her husband as a partner in her own self-denial. But from Evelyn's point of view, she was coping effectively. She developed a form of resistance that allowed her to rationalize the fact that her discretionary authority was eroding. From her point of view, she was fighting back. *She* was no floor mop! Or so she believed. As long as she believed it, she would go on practicing passive resistance, or abdicator behavior. Here is Evelyn's description of the way things were.

Evelyn: "I was always plainly told the orders of the day. My husband had been in the army. Well, I would smile very sweetly, after all I was a civilian, and say to myself, thank you very much but I am not in the army, and I would do my own thing once he was away. He used to tell me to take care of petty things, and I would say to myself, to hell with it, they would all be done in the normal course of events, and he probably wouldn't check on it anyway. When he walked in, he would lift the covers off the pots and pans on the stove, see what was cooking and then salt it. I just let him go ahead and do it, even though I had already salted it, and I had already made plans that if he made it inedible that was what he would be served. I let him suffer the consequences of his own acts. I always had an alternative in the background."

In this instance, the *abdicating behavior exhibited by Evelyn was lack of confrontation.* Understanding that avoiding confrontation is a way of abdicating is not sufficient if we want to be assured that issues that are important to us are brought into focus and if we are to treat the love relationship with the honesty it deserves. There are behavioral indicators that can, if we pay attention to them, cue us in to the fact that we are practicing *confrontation avoidance.*

Venting where it's safe is one of these indicators. Whether talking in frustration with a close friend or in tears with your mother or muttering under your breath while you're cooking dinner with the kids underfoot, the words are the same:

- "I don't have to put up with this," *but you do.*
- "I'm not taking this anymore," *but you do.*
- "This just isn't fair," *but you take no steps to correct it.*
- "He never wants to see my friends," *so you don't see them or go alone.*
- "He always says he'll do it, but he never follows through," *and neither do you.*

Venting where it's safe avoids action. Once vented, you feel better and the problem superficially appears to have been solved. The old cliché that women talk and men act may bear some looking into. There is little doubt that within the love relationship the abdicator who avoids confrontation often does so by confining her talking to safe environs. While venting where it's safe avoids confrontation with husband and lover, using humor as one discusses these complaints with one's friends allows the abdicator to hide her discontent from herself.

The *kidding on the square* that often creeps into our conversations to sugarcoat or somehow soften and withhold the truth is another signal that there is confrontation avoidance. Evelyn's "after all I am a civilian, . . . I am not in the army," and a comment from Elaine, whom you'll meet shortly, that "It didn't take a genius to figure out that at the rate of three credits per term it would take me twelve years to get my degree," are classic examples of kidding on the square. Evelyn didn't want to be ordered about and Elaine wanted to complete her degree as soon as possible, and both discussed their needs in jocular terms.

Venting where it's safe, the "wait 'til I tell my friends about this one" behavior, and handling discontent with humor intended to hide it are surefire signs of confrontation avoidance. It's easy to be adamant, to use strong language, and to give voice to difficulties in a nonchallenging situation.

It's easy. It's safe. It maintains the status quo. And it allows us to abdicate.

Given the almost unlimited variations of human behavior, it is not surprising that there are other methods when your goal is to avoid confrontation. Now let's meet Elaine, who chose a combination of *intellectual evasion* and *lying* as her coping technique.

At the time of the interview, she was forty-three years old and had long since experienced the rebirth from submissive wife to professional woman and single parent and was enthusiastically enjoying "that great big candy store out there called the world." During the early years of her marriage, she worked full time to support herself and her husband while he attended graduate school. She obtained her bachelor's degree by attending classes in the evenings and worked during the day. Within five years, they bought their first home, a great big Victorian house with enough ground around it and room inside it to keep her husband, Gary, outside mowing the lawn and Elaine inside waxing and polishing. At the same time they started on their required two children, new blue-and-white kitchen from Sears, and matching color schemes in the living room and dining room. Elaine was handy at wallpapering and stripping old wood. Gary, scientist that he was, "didn't know how to do those things."

Most of the women in the neighborhood joined the book club. Elaine joined the then New Democratic Coalition, made sandwiches for the kids who were keeping clean for Gene (McCarthy), hosted fund-raising soirees for the local congressman-to-be—it was the late Al Lowenstein, and he won—and became a committeewoman.

When Elaine wasn't busy keeping a spotless house, running to political meetings, or cooking for gourmet dinner parties, she tutored remedial students for the local school system and, of course, taught son number one how to read before he was four years old. Everything was great.

Life was going along as scheduled. And everything was just fine.

Until the divorce, eleven years after they were married. It

coincided, not all that coincidentally, with Elaine's entrance
into graduate school.

> *Elaine:* "I really felt that I had to be careful about the way I
> talked to Gary. He seemed to challenge just about every-
> thing I said. After a while, I began to get the hang of it. As
> long as I put things into a hypothetical framework, we
> wouldn't argue. Instead, we would discuss the relative
> benefits and possible negative consequences of whatever it
> was. Everything was intellectualized, analyzed as though
> it really wasn't a part of the two of us. It avoided argu-
> ments. But everything began to fall apart when we
> moved.
>
> "We first moved here so that my husband could take a
> sabbatical. I wanted to go back to school for a graduate
> degree. I discussed it with him and he said sure, go, but
> only take three credits. That way it wouldn't interfere
> with the chores, the children, and the house. Well, it didn't
> take a genius to figure out that if 72 credits are required
> for a doctorate, it would take twelve years to get it at that
> rate. I lied. I said OK and registered for fifteen credits
> instead of telling him. I used to put all my books in the
> laundry bag and pretend that I was going to the laundry.
> Then I finally ran away from home one weekend and went
> over to Janice's house. I made him take care of the kids,
> and I did the term papers that were due."

There's no doubt that Elaine was able to avoid arguments.
In the process, however, she also avoided discussing the real
issues in her marriage. Intellectual evasion, by making problems and concerns hypothetical, certainly has its uses. In the
work place, where honesty is often a matter of good judgment, the ability to talk about issues and concerns can save
you from tilting at windmills while you prepare yourself for
the important battles. In a marriage that is supposed to last
forever, using your intellect to avoid discussions of the areas
of your discontent prepares you for a lifetime of the same. It
also prepares you for the most active form of confrontation

avoidance—lying. The space between placing the shroud of your intellect over your discontent and lying is infinitesimal.

If our primary focus is to search for the "proper" way to describe our needs, we cannot help but put their true meaning and the intensity of our feelings in the background. We draw a circle, fill it with our needs, and then stalk it, taking ever so cautious jabs at it now and again, then drawing back when we sense the danger of honest confrontation.

Intellectual evasion is insidious. It allows the abdicator to hide her true feelings and desires not only from others but from herself as well. She becomes a virtuoso in the art of dissembling.

The behavioral cue to the use of intellectual evasion as a method of avoiding confrontation is easily recognized. If we preface what we are saying with "Let me see how to put this" or "I want to make sure that you understand what it is I'm saying," we are beginning the process of intellectual evasion. Certainly we should check on our language so that we are understood or so that we do not devastate the other person with verbal darts, but that is a far different monitoring system from the one used by the intellectual evader. Intellectual evasion removes the "I want," "I need," "I feel," "I believe." In doing so, the abdicator practicing intellectual evasion discounts and invalidates herself, her right to expression, and her discretionary authority over her environment.

In addition to refusing to confront the difference between their husbands' wishes and their own preferences, Evelyn and Elaine exhibited another often expressed behavior of the abdicator. *They viewed themselves as children* who were subject to being "checked up on" and who would, given the right set of circumstances, "run away from home." Evelyn avoided confrontation by keeping her actions to herself and not sharing her discontent. Elaine was more active in her approach and, expecting a negative response, pretended to acquiesce or used intellectual evasion, again a more active method of abdicating.

It is not my concern here to determine why Evelyn and Elaine abdicated. There are as many reasons why as there are women who practice abdication. *We do not need to know why we abdicate in order to effect the behavioral changes necessary to stop doing so.*

Certainly Evelyn did not come across as an abdicator outside of her marriage. No wimp she! You could look to Evelyn for leadership and direction off the homestead. There was a boundary beyond which she did not practice abdication. She was a closet abdicator. A generation later, Elaine found the same closet, and although more active in her approach, she too chose to abdicate. She was a political voice that commanded attention in her community, a "temporary" breadwinner supporting herself and her husband through school, a creative homemaker, an aggressor, *and* a closet abdicator.

What Evelyn and Elaine have in common is their inability to transfer their skills and behavior from their public lives to their personal lives. Evelyn lost confidence in her abilities as she allowed her behavior slowly to drain away her sense of self. Elaine lost hold of the sense of joy that she took in herself and her environment as she assigned away to her husband the right to determine more and more of her behavior. Both of these women delayed for a decade traveling the rites of passage from child to adult.

We can't ignore the difference in their methods. One practiced passive abdication, the other active abdication. This difference kept resurfacing as I collected other case histories, and as it did, I began to notice that it was generational. Younger women, those under forty, displayed active abdication, whereas older women were more passive. This distinction is particularly important to understand. Those of us who practice active abdication much more easily hide our acquiescent behavior from ourselves precisely because we think we are in control. We choose only from among *safe* actions. That is what we do not see.

Compare the profile of the passive abdicator with that of the active abdicator, and make note of the responses these two lists of attributes produce in you.

The Passive Abdicator

The passive abdicator practices don't-rock-the-boat behavior. She excuses her behavior by telling herself the following:

- "This may not be what I want, but then, since I don't know what position I would be in if I changed, I might just as well stay here."
- "It's better not to voice my disagreements."
- "Perhaps things aren't as bad as I think and maybe they will get better."
- "There really are no choices available."
- "If I am uncomfortable, at least I know the reasons for it."
- "I really can't do anything about it."
- "Most people stay in situations like this."
- "There are even some who would like to live the life I have."

The passive abdicator is apathetic in the search for new experiences and new life-styles.

- She is shy in new situations and attempts only a guided tour through her experiences.
- She gives credit to the "they say" authority.
- She subjects herself to paralysis through rationalization.
- She is among the last to effect new life-styles.
- She is never really satisfied with her physical appearance yet attempts little in the way of self-improvement.
- She prefers activities within the home to those outside of it.
- She is the last one to participate or to offer a suggestion or an idea.
- She is slow to respond to comments or statements outside of her environment.
- She sprinkles her language with modifying adjectives intended to soften and sugarcoat: "maybe," "perhaps," "somewhat," "a little."

- She does not understand implications beyond the spoken word.
- She lives and behaves on a superficial level.

The Active Abdicator

Here is the profile of the active abdicator:

- She lies rather than face confrontation.
- She is active in her discussions of her discontent, but only among those who have no power to change her realities and never with those who would challenge or criticize.
- If she isn't receiving sexual fulfillment at home, she is far more likely to take lovers than is her passive sister.
- She sees herself as strong; she chooses straw men to do battle with.
- She sees herself as determined, but only begins with a spate of energy and a flurry of activity and ends with rationalizations for not following through.
- She does many things well and few to completion.
- She sees herself as supportive, but she has hidden angers.
- She tells herself, "I got away with that one"; "Thank God he didn't find out"; "No one knows about it anyway."
- Her friends think her witty; she shrouds her discontent in humor.
- She sees herself as independent and yet rails at the forces that hold her back.
- She lobbies for freedom and she embraces security.

About one-third of the way through my research, I began to hold group discussions with women who agreed to share their experiences openly with one another as they had with me. Since many of them were relating events from their life histories that had occurred over a decade ago, hearing one another's stories helped trigger feelings that were long since dormant.

Evelyn and Elaine joined Ann, Carol, and Florence in one of these discussions. Elaine, Evelyn, and Ann all held graduate degrees. Carol had a bachelor's degree, and Florence had completed high school. Evelyn, Ann, and Florence were in their mid-fifties, Elaine in her early forties, and Carol was thirty-two. The topic of this particular discussion was, How have we abdicated and what did we give up in the process?

Ann: "I often abdicated when it came to confrontation because I knew that I wouldn't win. My husband was an attorney, he would win any disagreement that we had; he was trained to argue. I wasn't. I avoided all confrontation."

Elaine: "My husband had a right way to do everything— his way. He wanted me to dress a certain way, to talk a certain way, to walk a certain way. I remember him giving me instructions on how to laugh. He said that I laughed too loud and that I didn't laugh like a lady, and he demonstrated how I should laugh. He told me how to sleep, how to feel, what I should feel, how to make love, and how to act when he made love to me. He was a damned technician and he wanted me to be the robot. So I was."

Both Elaine and Ann voiced the question of whether or not they would ultimately have dissolved their marriages had they honestly confronted the difference between their preferences and their husbands' determination of how they should behave. Rather than risk the loss of an argument or a negative response, they chose to abdicate the issue.

In choosing to abdicate the issue, we have two background assumptions. First, that the issue is a win-lose situation where the woman must defer; and second, we are ascribing to the other person a negativism and even malice before there is proof of either.

Carol did not abdicate confrontation. Instead, *she abdicated the right to define herself.*

Carol: "I wanted approval and I didn't give myself approval. I wanted others to give it to me. I didn't feel okay unless someone else told me and then I would know that I was okay. I wanted my parents to approve the way I was living, I wanted my husband to approve what I was studying at school. I wanted my friends to approve of my husband. I wanted the butcher to approve of the meat I bought, and I wanted the guy at the bookstore to approve of the books I bought. I let other people originate the approval and I waited for them to verify it."

In relinquishing the right to define herself, the abdicator is without a sense of self-history and is unable to credit herself with her past accomplishments, thus limiting her ability to make choices and to create alternatives. In effect, this translates into her maintaining a situation that is in no way supportive of her growth. *Rather than seek the support she needs, she chooses to endure.*

The enduring behavior practiced by the abdicator is more subliminal in its intent and more passive than either avoidance or purposeful lying. Enduring usually requires rationalization of some kind. The abdicator may claim that she was unable to act in a situation for any number of seemingly plausible reasons—ill health, financial circumstances, other responsibilities. Placing the blame on the lack of permissive social norms ("No one else was doing what I was") is another rationalization for enduring. Whatever the rationalization, the abdicator is prevented from recognizing her self-worth and her abilities.

Having denied her own self-worth, the abdicator imbues her husband or lover with areas of expertise that she has no reason to assume he possesses. She relinquishes her right to discipline their children on the assumption that he is more capable. She relinquishes her right to participate in the handling of their finances on the assumption that he knows more about money. She relinquishes her right to choose a home on the assumption that he can handle it better. Men, no more than women, specifically prepare themselves for parenting, financial knowledge, or real estate acquisition, yet they are given the responsibilities in direct proportion to the degree that women relinquish them.

Evelyn and Florence told us how they gave up their financial well-being.

Evelyn: "I used all my savings to clothe myself and our son. When my husband took my car and sold it, I signed all the papers, and he went out and bought himself a stereo that he took with him when we finally got the divorce. Then to top it all off, I worked literally for nothing all those years when I could have been building up money for myself or getting on with my career."

Florence: "I overcompensated in my second marriage for what my first husband had accused me of. My first husband said that I wasn't affectionate enough and that I never gave him anything."

Florence was married the first time to a naval officer, who allowed his alcoholism to interfere with his wife and daughter. Yet in face of that, Florence accepted his definition of her inabilities.

Florence: "In my second marriage I gave my husband unbounded affection, anything he wanted. I did everything for him. I gave him gifts. He used me to get what he wanted and I let him. Before we were married, I put all my savings into a home that we were building and used most of my assets. That turned out to be foolish. My divorce decree was not yet final, but we had the ceremony anyway. He told me that if we had to wait for a final decree we would just get married again. About two weeks after the ceremony my final decree came. We were living together in the house that was built mostly with my money. When I told him that we had to get married again, he said, 'Well, what do you want me to do about it!' I should have told him to get out, but I didn't. I knew he had no conscience, but I didn't even listen to what I knew about him. I loved him enough that I thought I could sacrifice and live with that type of attitude. There was no legal recourse for me—the house was in both of our names and I wasn't even married to him. Eventually, as our relationship eroded, he took more and more of my financial assets."

Florence settled for less than she wanted and got it. As for her live-in companion, he subscribed to the "Blessed are the meek for they give me what I want" philosophy. Florence concentrated on a three-sided pattern of abdicating behavior, including the willingness to "sacrifice," the acceptance of another person's authority as to which behaviors were appropriate, and the surrender of financial responsibility.

The willingness to sacrifice is a condition that always follows compromise. It is not so much that each act of sacrifice is so devastating. For example, moving to another town because of his career may not be so great a sacrifice—but what happens when *your* opportunities require a move? Going out with his friends is not so great a sacrifice—but what about seeing *your* friends? Listening to his complaints and fears about his work is not so great a sacrifice—but what about when you want to talk about *your* concerns? Making love when you really don't feel like it is not so great a sacrifice—but what about making love when *he* doesn't feel like it? *It is the pattern of self-denial that turns compromise into sacrifice.*

The abdicator who has accepted the role of primary compromiser usually does so in the beginning of her relationship. A pattern of behavior is set in motion with one compromise leading to another. The compromises she makes begin to form an unwritten contract between her and her husband that clearly distinguishes between acceptable and unacceptable behaviors and activities.

After a period of time, the limits the abdicator allows to be placed on her behavior extend to her attitudes about self and her relationship to the rest of her environment. The dreams and ambitions, the sense of self and plans of "What I'm going to do, be, have, when I grow up" have disappeared. Her personal goals to achieve positions of authority both at home and in the work place have been laid aside. Sacrifice has replaced compromise. Middle age and quiet despair have replaced youth and enthusiasm.

Florence accepted her first husband as an authority on what was behaviorally appropriate for her, in spite of the fact that he was an alcoholic. In handing over this authority, she relinquished her right to learn. True affection is earned, and care and consideration in adult relationships are meted out in equal measure. To give more than you receive gives tacit agreement to inequality. When you sign away ownership of your emotions and feelings, you lose sight of your needs and thus cause them not to be met. These three areas are the behavioral mainstays of the abdicator:

1. Relinquishing the right to learn
2. Unequal offerings of care and consideration
3. Assigning the emotional content of the self to another

Florence relinquished financial responsibility, perhaps believing that a concern about protecting what belonged to her would be indicative of mistrust or unloving behavior. In a relationship, whether it is sanctioned by marriage or not, women need to disassociate money and financial security from love. They need to handle it themselves and behave as adults. To do otherwise is to commit abdication.

In spite of all the talk warning women to be wise about their money, too many of them don't listen. And this refusal to listen is due to the belief that they don't have the right of ownership over what they earn when they work or the belief that they are not contributing to the household in their roles as homemakers. Not believing in the right of ownership is

another product of self-denial. Why, after all, should we be
"smart" about money when we haven't been "smart" about
equality in love?

Another of Florence's comments bears mention here: "I
didn't even listen to what I knew about him." Love and
passion always come equipped with rose-colored glasses, and
all of us would do well to take them off on a regular basis so
that we can pragmatically assess the assets and debits of our
relationships. To do otherwise is to receive less than what
you both want and deserve.

The ultimate result of the practice of abdicator behavioral
patterns within the love relationship is that the woman *as
abdicator maintains a relationship in spite of a de-escalation of her
stated needs and desires.*

- She maintains a relationship in order to keep what she
  insists she does not want.
- She chooses security in place of freedom.
- She chooses acquiescence in place of equality.
- She chooses endurance in place of responsibility.
- She keeps no tally sheet of pain and pleasure, of discon-
  tent and satisfaction, of indifference and companion-
  ship, of fear and security.

In the absence of a mental tally sheet and the keeping of
historical records of the relationship, the abdicator requires
an authority figure—a doctor or therapist—to help her move
away from any relationship, no matter how damaging, instead of taking a leadership role in her own life. You will
understand exactly what I mean about keeping a tally sheet—
you will know how to keep one—before you finish reading
this book.

Chapter Four

From Acquiescence to Equality

*In days gone by, when you were out
I'd open the window and give a shout
I could laugh and I could sing and
in my soul such bells would ring
then you'd come in and open the door
and say, "Do not sing anymore."
Why?*

—Elaine

"I wrote that when I was going through my divorce. That's why I had to get away," Elaine told me. "I just didn't feel joy anymore. It took so much energy to hide who I really was from my husband."

It takes energy and it takes strength. Strength to move toward self-determination and independently created behaviors. When these forces—the energy level, strength, and the drive—are pulled together, they are perceived as a total behavior pattern that sets the woman displaying it apart from the group of which she is a member.

It is at the point of separating that a kind of trial begins; a drama in which the newborn bitch is tried by a jury of those whose interest in her abdicator status is now threatened. Whereas as abdicator the woman plays the role of the primary compromiser, the move toward self-determination requires that she place limits on the compromises she is willing to make. Whether she exercises these limits consciously or subliminally, she begins the process of becoming a bitch.

Joyce: "I became so angry at being told what to do by my husband, even though I essentially asked to be told. I was giving out clues that said you tell me so I'll do it right. You tell me so I'll fit in. You tell me so I'll be loved. You tell me, whatever, just fill in the blanks, just you tell me. I even complied with it and agreed to it. Every time I felt angry, I called myself a bitch, as I am sure other people around me did. In a way I feel that the anger was a very positive experience because it gave me energy instead of the depression that compliance made me feel. When I was in compliance, I didn't act; when I was angry, I took control, and I defined taking control as being a bitch."

Joyce, at twenty-eight, was one of the younger women taking part in a group discussion that focused on the feelings and emotions generated when the choice between other-determined and self-determined behavior is being made. She voiced the primary emotional contrast: depression for the abdicator and anger for the bitch. The next thing to be understood was that the *subliminal* response for the abdicator was anger (accompanied by confusion); the subliminal response for the bitch was anxiety.

Moving out of the abdicator role and into the bitch role can occur as the result of a specific event, a process, a discussion with a friend, or a new activity or experience. But for the majority of women I interviewed, the movement was the result of happenstance. It was unplanned, and as a result, the movement took longer to accomplish, and the emotional content was draining. For the very few of the women who planned and calculated the movement, the result was a quicker determination of self-worth.

Here are the stories of three women whose histories mirror those of many of the women I interviewed. Joann is fifty-seven; Diane, thirty-two; and Gloria, forty-seven.

Joann

The finishing touches to the renovation of Lillie Langtry's Restaurant had just been completed. Joann, a co-owner with her son, was directing an on-site commercial that was being taped for cable television. She made a last dash to retrieve a pumpkin that decorated the bar area in celebration of the fall season, shouting, "Get that out of there! We'll want to use this tape to cover our promotions throughout the year."

Then she sat down with me at a table from which she could have a clear view of the camera and follow the footage being shot. Rarely a smoker, she took one of my cigarettes. Her grown daughter came over, set some drinks in front of us, and left.

"We've only been open three weeks. I know we're not supposed to break even for a while, but that doesn't stop me from worrying about it," Joann told me. Three months ago she backed her son, Mike, putting up her home as collateral for the note to purchase Lille Langtry's. With the renovations, if it were sold today, they would make a 50 percent profit. Since the plan was to operate a successful restaurant, even that knowledge did little to quell her anxiety. Mike is the operating owner; Joann serves as silent partner.

With a full-time public relations job, Joann is also vice-president of a prestigious professional association for the

Midwest region, a past president and still active member of the American Cancer Society, and a newly elected board member of a citizens' action organization. She is also the recipient of several national awards as well as being listed in *Who's Who of American Women* and the *International Biography of Women.* Yet Joann somehow manages to handle all the restaurant's promotion and advertising and give more than a silent partner's share of advice on pricing, payroll, and a new lunch menu.

Lillie Langtry's wasn't the first risk Joann had taken. The first risk was her decision to end a twenty-year marriage. Now, seven years after the divorce, Joann recalls the incident that triggered the first risk and started her on the move from acquiescence to equality.

Joann: "You know, I can remember the very day when I refused to accept my husband's definition of me as a bitch. It's very clear to me because I was at home for twelve years with four children. When my youngest son was in kindergarten, I was offered a part-time position in public relations and I took it. Well, I discussed it with my husband first, and he said, 'Are you sure you're going to be able to manage everything?' And I said, 'Oh, sure, I can do everything.' You know, no problem. At that time I was working only three mornings a week and my son was in a car pool. Well, one day my son came home about one minute before I did and he had a friend with him, and my husband had come home to check. He often came home to check up at noon. He was checking up to see that everything was all right, that I was there, and that I was doing everything that I was supposed to do and that his children were all right. For some reason he completely exploded, just exploded and called me a bitch and a whore, said that I was abdicating my responsibility and there had been no clue up to that point. He just got hysterical and ranted and raved and screamed and stomped out of the house and I stood there dumbfounded. I had always been very agreeable to everything he said, and I always said fine. But at that point something clicked, like a light bulb going off in my head, and I said, but I'm not a bitch. From that point on I looked at things differently, more critically, and for my own development."

For Joann, it was this single event that forced her to reexamine her husband's definition of her behavior and his expectations of her actions. She brought to the surface her subliminal awareness that his actions of "checking up" directly implied that he did not view her as a bona fide and responsible adult. That his designation of her as a bitch meant that whenever she stepped out of the role he had determined she should play, she was a bitch.

Diane

The dinner table was set for a buffet for eight. Waterford crystal and blue and cranberry-flowered Wedgwood china graced the sideboard that was placed against a whitewashed brick wall in the kitchen area that bordered the dining room. Diane poured us some coffee, and we went to sit in the living room that was ready to receive her guests. As she placed the napkins in front of us, it was obviously a gesture of both concern for the table and pride in the appointments of her home. An eclectic selection of antiques blended well with the ultramodern renovation that her apartment had undergone.

Diane, almost as fragile-looking as her crystal, is a petite blond. Her work belies her appearance. With a graduate degree in business, Diane works as a management consultant, designing and implementing productivity improvement programs. Each of her assignments is worth hundreds of thousands of dollars to her company, and her own services are billed out at over $5,000 a week. She meets with chief executives on a daily basis and is often a key figure in closing the sale of her company's services.

After a five-year on-again, off-again affair with a married man, Diane transferred her aggressiveness from her business life to her personal life and made the decision to end the affair. In the process, she changed her self-image and developed a healthy sense of self-worth.

Diane: "For many years I thought of myself as a second-stringer. I have always been ambitious, and there was always another step up the ladder that I wanted to climb. Good, better, best, never let it rest, until the good gets better and the better gets best. That was my attitude. The problem was that I always let others grade me. When I gave my lover an ultimatum that he would have to choose between me and his marriage and he decided to stay with his wife, I was devastated. During the relationship I had gained a lot of weight, and I was always at his beck and call. When I began to ask for more of his time, he would ask me how he could arrange it. Could I get a friend to lend us a car, could I think of an excuse that he could give to his wife, could I pick up something for dinner or for brunch? After we split, I realized that I had been setting up a fantasy for him and for myself as well. I was waiting for something to happen, and I was the one who had to make it happen. I was in a holding pattern. After we broke up, the weight seemed to melt off. I finally went about redecorating my apartment and began thinking of myself as an individual. All of a sudden I wasn't a second-stringer anymore."

Diane made the move to self-determination by confronting her needs and wants, accepting the consequences, and moving forward. An important step in initiating this move was her awareness that the demands made on her by her lover exceeded the effort he was willing to put forth. Once she recognized this as a pattern in their relationship, she began to limit the compromises she had been making in order to maintain the affair. With the dissolution of the affair, it was all the more evident that its disruption was due primarily to the removal of her support. Diane had, indeed, during the five-year term of their affair "been setting up a fantasy for him and for myself as well."

Whether through chance or a planned action, the abdicator becoming a bitch must consciously recognize that she was born into a world created by others and therefore she must make her own history and her own personal realities. Should she wish a reality different from the one offered to her, she must transform, through her actions, her very perception of her history. In moving from acquiescence to equality, from abdicator to bitch, a sense of self-history and an appreciation of past accomplishments are imperative.

Without exception, women who had abdicated during the love relationship encountered great difficulty in developing a healthy appreciation of self. They neglected to focus on their own history of work, home management, and other areas of their lives where they *had* been self-directed. They kept no ledger of their past accomplishments, and in the absence of a pragmatic and realistic sense of self-worth and ability, they allowed their spouses to remove their discretionary authority.

When they began to take the practical steps toward equality, they initiated the process of recognizing their self-worth on an intellectual level. By the time they had completed the steps necessary to gain equality, they had learned to appreciate themselves on an emotional level as well.

Those first practical steps were all aimed at self-improvement, some of it needed and some not. Activities ranged from diets, getting new hairstyles, and changes in the manner of dress to taking I.Q. tests, applying for membership in professional societies, joining community organizations and taking leadership roles, taking course work, and getting additional degrees. These women were out to prove to themselves that they were capable and deserving. They put all their efforts into developing self-pride, and they did themselves proud.

Gloria

According to Gloria, her physical appearance before and after her separation would make her a prime candidate for a diet commercial. When I met her, there was certainly no trace of the "before" picture. Slim, vivacious, and well-turned-out in her designer jeans, she led me into the front room of her ten-room home in an older residential section of town. At forty-seven, Gloria had lived two lives, one in which she had put her life on hold and relegated herself to a limbo of acquiescence bordering on subservience, and one in which she lived life on her own.

Newly married, she supported her husband through his internship in surgery. Grueling though those years were, Gloria glowed with confidence and energy as she bore her first child followed in quick succession by the next three, held down a full-time job, and ran her household and her life with precision-honed organization.

Gloria: "When we were first married, I had the highest-paying public relations job in the city. We had a great apartment. We even had air conditioning, and that's when nobody had it. My husband was still doing his internship, so I was supporting us. Well, we had the first four of the children, and I only took two weeks off for each of them. I had a housekeeper; I kept my job. I was not overburdened at home; I managed it all. I certainly supported more than my half of our living expenses. Later, after our fifth child, when my husband finished his internship and I quit my job because it was supposed to be temporary, it all went downhill. When he asked for a separation, I didn't think I could do anything. I was economically dependent. All of a sudden I couldn't handle anything. I had to go back for my master's degree before I could feel capable again."

Gloria did more than just become capable again. With a degree in liberal arts, a master's in history, and an excellent track record in public relations, she won a position as director of public relations for a Fortune 500 firm. These actions, which she initiated on her own, changed the balance of her relationship with her husband to the point where it was no longer tipped on his side.

Gloria: "Doug and I met for drinks about six months after I was made director of P.R. The best thing I was able to bring to our meeting was the fact that, dammit, I had been taking care of *me,* my kids, and my work and doing very well at it. All the old questions and suggestions and directions were not only absurd from my point of view, they were somehow unnecessary from Doug's point of view as well. He said, 'You don't need me to tell you what to do anymore. And believe me, it was hard work—I never liked it. But what do you want me for?' Well, I told him I wanted him as a lover, I wanted him as a husband, I wanted him to pick up some of the slack in the household chores. I wanted to live with him! But I also wanted to live with myself . . ."

Doug's realization that it had been hard work telling Gloria what to do and that he was now released from the responsibility of running another person's life was an important component in bringing them back together as two equal partners.

Joann, Diane, and Gloria, all talented, bright, and with above-average potential to lead fulfilling lives, spent among the three of them a total of forty years playing the role of abdicator before they recognized the consequences of their behavior and took the steps to break the pattern of acquiescence. *They didn't have to wait that long!*

Chapter Five

The Three-Step Process

From their stories and through their experiences and the experiences of the many women who have shared their histories with me and with one another, we can separate out a three-step process that will, if practiced, move the abdicator immediately toward equality and away from the pathway to self-denial.

The invalidation and the discounting encountered by women are both historical fact and public issue. They do not become an individual issue until the woman's personal biography forces her to come into direct conflict with the behaviors imposed on her by others and which she has willingly assumed. Put more bluntly, when sexism affects you on a personal level, you experience conflict. *This becomes the point of choice: either to abdicate or to wear the culturally defined label of bitch, as one moves from acquiescence to equality in the love relationship, from weakness to strength in parenting, and from compliance to authority within work affiliations.*

If the abdicator is to move away from self-denial, then she must do so within her total behavioral framework. It is not sufficient to speak up for oneself on a special occasion or to insist on the next major purchase or to let him "see what I have to put up with for a change." These are Band-Aid approaches and will not break the self-denial pathway. Isolated events do not serve as dominoes in establishing relationships to break the pattern. The entire pattern must be rearranged. It is for this reason that it becomes important to view the abdicator's behavior as a pathway, to describe those behaviors, to recognize the impact they have on oneself and on others, and to practice the interference techniques that can break the self-denial pathway.

To begin the process, here are the steps the abdicator must follow:

Step I Recognize the behavior
Step II Understand its impact
Step III Practice interference techniques

DIAGRAM 1. The Abdicator's Pathway to Self-Denial

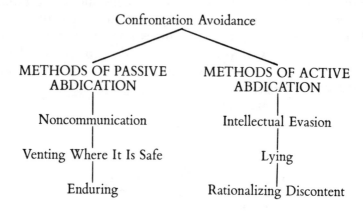

Confrontation Avoidance

METHODS OF PASSIVE ABDICATION | METHODS OF ACTIVE ABDICATION

Noncommunication

Venting Where It Is Safe

Enduring

Intellectual Evasion

Lying

Rationalizing Discontent

BEHAVIORS PRACTICED IN BOTH PASSIVE AND ACTIVE ABDICATION

Assuming Win-Lose Outcome

Assuming Malicious Intent

Use of Humor to Hide Discontent

Childlike Behavior

Unrealistic Assumption of Partner's Abilities

Lack of Realistic Sense of Self-history

De-escalation of Expressed Needs, Wants, and Desires

Result: Maintenance of Unfulfilling Relationships

The Abdicator's Pathway to Self-Denial

Diagram 1 reflects the abdicator's pathway to self-denial. The pathway begins with confrontation avoidance and the differences between active and passive methods used to avoid communication of our needs, wants, and desires. The remaining behaviors that are practiced, unfortunately with equal success by both the active and passive abdicator, begin with assuming win-loss outcomes and continue through the de-escalation of expressed needs, wants, and desires. The sum total of these behaviors is the same whether we practice active or passive abdication—the maintenance of unfulfilling relationships.

It might be helpful to recall the case histories reported in previous sections where the abdicating behaviors were first introduced in order to insure a firm understanding of what is meant by each of them.

The Three-Step Process Toward Equality

The next section outlines the Three-Step Process toward Equality and lets us see at a glance each of the behaviors, their impact, and the interference techniques used to offset the behavior.

Before getting into a full description of the process, a word of encouragement and of caution.

The behavioral techniques that run interference with the abdicator's pathway to self-denial require no therapy, no unusual soul-searching, and no complex special training in order to implement them. Much as the actor learns how to project a given set of emotions and feelings on the screen with her language, body movements, voice inflections, and expressions, so also can we learn behavioral techniques that either cause us to relinquish control or permit us to take control over our environment. The choice to implement these techniques is yours.

You can only exercise that choice, however, if you practice the techniques. Some of these techniques require you to make lists of your needs and wants as well as reactions to past behavior. Some require you to be objective and pragmatic, whereas others require you to be introspective in order to identify your feelings and emotions. Because learning likes company and practice requires it, some techniques involve sharing your lists and answers with lovers and husbands and family and friends. All of them require thought, and all require honesty. It is especially important to complete the exercises provided.

Note: Read the table that follows once, understanding it as best you can. Then read the section immediately after it—the explanation of the table. Read that section very slowly. Then return to the table and read it through once again. At that point, stop and think about what you have read before going further.

It is helpful to read this section with a group and discuss with one another the ways in which you can apply the methods to your situation. Whenever possible, challenge your own behavior where you recognize similarities. The best way to be kind to yourself is to be candid about your past behavior.

Imagine yourself confronting your partner and role-play future conversations. Write them out and play them as you would a script.

Share the techniques with your partner. You need his help and his thinking to get feedback on your behavior and your concerns. Pick your sharing time carefully and share slowly, not all at once. Communication patterns that have become habits are not broken overnight. Both the practice of the techniques and the results they allow take time.

TABLE 1. THE THREE-STEP PROCESS TOWARD EQUALITY

Step I: Recognizing Abdicating Behavior	Step II: Understanding the Impact	Step III: Practicing Interference Techniques
1. Non-communication	Hiding needs from others	• Use "I" message • Get commitment from partner to listen • Rely on your authority
2. Venting where it is safe	False assumption of problem solving	• Confront safe behavior with your friends • Use bitch sessions to set up action plans
3. Enduring	Martyrdom	• Get feedback regarding emotional content of communication • Listen actively to partner's needs
4. Intellectual evasion	Habitual dissembling	• Get feedback regarding pragmatic content of communication • Get partner to summarize your point of view • Check for understanding
5. Lying	Escalates conflict	• Select your most recent and least important lie and tell the truth
6. Rationalizing discontent	Loss of "I" message	• Use "I" message • Follow through on "they" message
7. Assuming win-lose outcome	Setting up for failure	• Define objective • Set up action plan • Present objective, action plan, and consequences to partner • Implement action plan

Step I: Recognizing Abdicating Behavior	Step II: Understanding the Impact	Step III: Practicing Interference Techniques
8. Assuming malicious intent	Fosters hostility	• Check your understanding • Check your emotional content • Recognize withdrawal behaviors
9. Use of humor to hide discontent	Sugarcoats needs, wants, and desires	• Get feedback • Check emotional content of communication
10. Childlike behavior	Relinquishes adult rights and privileges	• Check "double standard" issues
11. Unrealistic assumption of partner's abilities	Relinquishes discretionary authority	• Challenge partner's knowledge sources • Initiate self-study • Actively seek opinions of recognized experts
12. Lack of realistic sense of self-history	Limits self-growth and potential	• List past accomplishments • List positive comments • Review lists for skills and characteristics • Review lists for emotional content
13. De-escalation of needs, wants, and desires	Sets up non-negotiable lifestyle	• Initiate and maintain needs-wants ledger

Understanding the Three-Step Process toward Equality

1. Recognizing Abdicating Behavior: Noncommunication

Keeping areas of discontent to oneself.

Understanding the Impact

The impact of noncommunication is to hide needs, wants, and desires from others, and it begins the process of de-escalating expressed needs and desires.

Practicing Interference Techniques

- Begin the communication with the "I message." I want, I feel, I believe.
- Get a commitment from your partner to understand that you are going to talk about how you feel, and get his commitment that he is willing to listen to your feelings, your reasons, and your point of view. Don't begin to explain your point of view until you have his commitment to listen. If you present your views before getting the commitment to listen, you will be talking at, not with, your partner.
- Stay away from phrases like "it appears," "they think," "other people do it," "Sally's husband lets her." You are talking about your relationship, and to rely on the authority and actions of others is to remove your discretionary authority as well as to bring in extraneous material that can throw you off the track.

2. Recognizing Abdicating Behavior: Venting where it is safe

The discussion of problems, concerns, and issues with those who have no power to affect the situation, while avoiding confrontation with the partner in the love relationship.

Understanding the Impact

Venting or talking out a problem generally removes some of the intensity surrounding it. It brings feelings and emotions to the surface, leaving the individual with a sense of security. The major impact is that the abdicator who vents only where it is safe and where no confrontation occurs, experiences counterfeit not actual security. Counterfeit security leaves the individual with the belief that the problem has been solved.

In addition, we take with us the perspective that "It can't be all that bad. My friends have similar situations." Venting where it is safe engenders a misery-likes-company approach to problem solving, while the issue causing the misery remains unsolved.

Practicing Interference Techniques

- The gripe or bitch sessions that safe venting allows require an open confrontation with your friends if you are to move the area of discussion to the proper place for the battle. Most of us are aware when we are complaining to the wrong people, and it takes only that admission and the inviting of feedback from your group to break safe venting behavior.
- In addition to inviting feedback regarding your complaints, use these sessions to set up an action plan to confront the issues with your partner and to allow you to take greater control. We have had the benefits of consciousness raising in the seventies. The eighties will only benefit from this awareness if action results.

3. Recognizing Abdicating Behavior: Enduring

To endure is to suffer overtly without yielding in the face of either real or imaginary hardships. The abdicator practicing this behavior is willing to sacrifice for just about any needy, and some not so needy, cause that comes into her environment. The posture of enduring allows the abdicator to avoid responsibility for changing her situation.

Understanding the Impact
The impact of enduring behavior is felt in every aspect of the abdicator's family relationships and by all members within it, husband and children alike. Her behavior causes guilt in varying degrees in all of them as she engages in martyrdom.

Most family members find it exceedingly difficult to counter the stoicism associated with enduring behavior precisely because of its passive nature, which causes them feelings of entrapment. Ultimately, partners and children find few techniques barring escalation of conflict and increased hostility to deal with this behavior.

Practicing Interference Techniques
The abdicator practicing enduring behavior needs to be provided with cues so that she can recognize that she expresses enduring behavioral patterns.

- Some of these cues are repeated apologies offered by other family members on one extreme, and bursts of anger with no specific cause on the other extreme. Either one of these behaviors from other family members should be responded to with questions that ask for information about the concerns and feelings of family members.
- Whereas in intellectual evasion the abdicator requires feedback with respect to the pragmatic content of her behavior, in enduring behavior the abdicator requires feedback regarding the emotional content of her behavior.

4. Recognizing Abdicating Behavior: Intellectual evasion
The use of words and phrases intended to subvert both the accuracy and intensity of feelings, needs, wants, and desires. The active simulation of counterfeit emotions and actions with the intent to mask true emotional content.

Understanding the Impact
- The abdicator practicing intellectual evasion eventually hides her needs from herself as well as from her partner. This increases the conflict that she experiences between her actual behavior and the behavior she wishes to express. She may impress her partner as bright and intellectual or as shrewd, calculating, and manipulative, depending upon his perception.

Practicing Interference Techniques
- It is difficult to catch yourself at what might be a habitual communication pattern. For this reason the intellectual evader must utilize a technique that will invite feedback to what she has said.
- Asking your partner to summarize your statements and to give you his understanding of how you feel provides that feedback. When you hear that your comments have caused your partner to underestimate the intensity of your true feelings, you are in a better position to recognize the practice of intellectual evasion.
- Getting the other person to summarize also allows you to check on his understanding of what you have said.
- When you recognize that you have a tendency to communicate in a certain fashion and you are attempting to break the pattern, confronting the pattern openly with your partner and enlisting his aid and his perceptual abilities to help you recognize it as it is occurring will help you to practice more accurate and effective communication.
- Inviting feedback, checking for understanding, and confronting old communication patterns give you an instant replay of the interaction and effectively interfere with the denial of honest feelings and emotions.

5. Recognizing Abdicating Behavior: Lying
The telling of a falsehood in order to be able to get your way without having to confront the situation. The liar

either consciously or subliminally considers herself to be the weaker partner. In effect, her behavior is to say, "I don't have the strength to tell the truth or to accept the consequences."

Understanding the Impact
The impact of lying is to escalate the conflict, not because you place yourself in the position of being caught, but because the outward practice of acquiescence allows greater and greater chasms to develop between you and your partner. If the truth of your needs, feelings, desires, and wants has to be disguised, you are aiding and abetting the de-escalation of those needs.

Disguising the truth causes you to maintain a relationship that you do not want for a period of time that is longer than necessary.

A secondary impact of lying is that when you find it necessary you are effectively telling yourself that your partner has more authority than you do—not equal authority. Here again, you begin to lose your discretionary authority over your environment as well as evidencing childlike behavior.

Practicing Interference Techniques
- Lying differs from other abdicating behavior in that we need no help in recognizing that we are using the method. The most useful, and only available, method to interfere with the practice of lying is to tell the truth.
- It is hardly advisable to mount a mammoth confession if you have used this technique as a habitual behavior pattern during your relationship. This could be disastrous.
- The method suggested here is to select your most recent and least important lie, confront it with your partner, discuss why you felt it was important to withhold the truth, and accept the consequences. Once you break the lying pattern in lesser issues, it

becomes easier to confront honestly concerns that have greater impact in your relationship.

6. Recognizing Abdicating Behavior: Rationalizing discontent
Putting blame for discontent on events or individuals outside of or unconnected to the relationship.

Understanding the Impact
The impact of rationalizing personal discontent is the loss of the "I" message. The abdicator will say, for example, "They don't do it that way," or "That's the way it's done," instead of saying, "I want to do it this way because . . ." or "My method is to . . ."

The partner gains the impression that his spouse or lover has a need to gain approval from individuals whose wishes and choices should not affect the relationship. In addition, the loss of the "I" message leaves the other partner with the impression that his mate requires the concurrence of others before trust will be accorded him.

Practicing Interference Techniques
- Include the "I" message, "I want," "I feel," "I think," in your communication pattern. In addition, follow through on the "they message" that you have been using.
- Give your partner information as to why you feel he is right or his actions are the best. Simply to state that others may have an answer or a solution is not sufficient.
- Your partner in the love relationship deserves the best of your analytical ability and the best of your complete thinking regarding issues and concerns that confront you both.

7. Recognizing Abdicating Behavior: Assuming a win-lose outcome
The assumption here is that only one partner can win. It

is based on the belief that there are no available compromises or that the woman must assume a greater burden of compromise should one be available. A secondary assumption is that the need being expressed will necessarily be met with a negative response from the other partner.

Understanding the Impact
The impact of this behavior is to set oneself up for failure. In addition, assumptions about another's response will, if incorrect, prevent you from understanding and gaining increased knowledge about your partner.

When a negative response does result and that response is related only to a denial of what you want for yourself, instead of a reaction your partner has to the impact your behavior might have on the relationship you share with him, then you need to understand that on a conscious level. Specific examples would be your wish to change jobs, go to school, join a political party, attend a social function—you fill it in—and these activities ask no more of your partner than that he has asked or you have given.

When the abdicator denies herself this knowledge, she keeps information about her partner on a subliminal level and she moves farther away from equality within the relationship.

Practicing Interference Techniques
Phase I
- Examine and define your objective clearly.
- Don't present ill-conceived and partially defined objectives.
- Your partner in the love relationship deserves the effort of your intellect as much as your supervisor in a work relationship does.
- Presenting a clear objective prevents the introduction of extraneous material.

Phase II   ● Set up an action plan to accomplish your objective.

● When you reach this point in your discussion, you should be talking about how you are to accomplish your objective, not whether you ought to attempt it.

Phase III   ● Present your objective, action plan, and the consequences that carrying out your plan will have on your relationship.

● Present only one point at a time, checking periodically to make sure your partner understands.

● Compare and contrast the areas where you agree and where you disagree.

Phase IV   ● Take action to carry out your plan. The bona fide and responsible adult takes responsibility for her own well-being and for her own actions.

● These techniques presuppose a rationality of both your approach and of the attitudes and behavior of your partner.

● If the response that you receive is bizarre and neurotic behavior, such as physical or mental abuse, then obviously this is not a relationship that should be maintained.

● It should be emphasized here that we are not talking about neurotically symbiotic relationships. Our focus here is on the love relationship that fits within the range of normalcy but which, given sociocultural realities of the past, has caused women to express abdicating behavior.

8. Recognizing Abdicating Behavior: Assuming malicious intent

Ascribing to your partner covert and negative reasons for his behavior, actions, and responses.

Understanding the Impact
Prejudging malice escalates hostility and prevents open communication.

It leads the abdicator who practices this behavior to assume win-lose outcomes. It prevents her from understanding her partner's reasons and allows her to hide the degree of dissension between her and her partner from herself. Frequently the problem is not malice but the status quo.

Practicing Interference Techniques
● Check your understanding and check your feelings. Most of us are aware when our discontent is causing us to withdraw from our partners.

● Withdrawal can take the form of withholding sexual pleasures to preparing a food we know is disliked, to preferring company outside of the relationship, to insisting that outings always include others. These behaviors are cues that you do not expect a fair hearing or pleasurable companionship within the relationship when you and your partner are not interacting with others.

● Keep a running check on your withdrawal behavior. This check may show you that you may be prejudging your partner. Once you are aware of the type and frequency of your withdrawal behaviors, you are in a position to confront them openly both with yourself and your partner.

9. Recognizing Abdicating Behavior: Use of humor to hide discontent
The use of humor to imply that oneself is not deserving or that the complaint has no validity. In addition to directing this behavior to themselves, abdicators who practice it also direct it toward their partners, implying a condescension or a lack of capability. Some of the best examples of self-directed condescension can be heard in Joan Rivers's comedy routines, while other-directed put-

downs are expressed in the Don Rickles type of humor.
Both may be fine on the stage to be laughed at, but they
are inappropriate when used to avoid confrontation or to
express true needs within the love relationship.

Understanding the Impact

The impact of this type of behavior is to sugarcoat or
soften the intensity of needs, wants, and desires. The
individual practicing the behavior is still fully aware of
the degree of her discontent and often wonders why her
partner missed the point.

If she ascribes to her partner a purposeful lack of
understanding, the conflict is escalated to the point
where she is left with a full-scale hostile confrontation as
the only means with which to voice her needs.

If she ascribes a lack of understanding that is not purposeful to her partner, she comes to accept his inability
and begins the process of enduring, thus contributing to
a de-escalation of her expressed needs.

Practicing Interference Techniques

- Here again, in order to counter an established behavior
  pattern, feedback is required.
- If being witty is one of the trademarks of your communication pattern, there is a good chance, if you
  have practiced additional abdicating behavior, that
  you use humor to cloak the intensity of your feelings.
- Open confrontation with your partner: a discussion of
  whether this is occurring in your interactions. Getting
  his commitment to check for the emotional content
  possibly hidden in your humor can effectively break
  this pattern.

10. Recognizing Abdicating Behavior: Childlike behavior

The underlying assumption of childlike behavior is that
you are subject to the restraints of authority over and
above those your partner is subject to. Any behavior that

represents an inequality of decision making or limits the activities of one while allowing these same activities for the other, causes the partner under these restraints to be treated as a child. Acceptance of the restraints reflects childlike behavior.

Understanding the Impact
The abdicator within the love relationship who practices childlike behavior relinquishes her right and privileges as an adult. In addition, she places additional responsibilities on her partner, forcing him to assume unilateral responsibility in those areas where she has abdicated.

Practicing Interference Techniques
● The abdicator practicing childlike behavior has been acquiescing to double standards within her relationships. Rather than confront them, she has chosen to ask permission as a substitute for initiating her own actions.
● If all issues were confronted at once, it would only serve to escalate the conflict. Choose the issue that is the most important to your needs and wants. Once you have chosen the issue that you will use to interfere with the behavior, follow through on the techniques suggested for the abdicator who assumes win-lose outcomes.

11. **Recognizing Abdicating Behavior: Unrealistic assumption of partner's abilities**
Ascribing to one's partner expertise, knowledge, ability, or experience in any given area without legitimization in the form of prior experience, past accomplishments, or specific study.

Understanding the Impact
The unrealistic assumption of another's ability causes the individual to relinquish her discretionary authority, thus permitting her to accept inequality in the relationship. In

addition, it gives her partner a mistaken view of his abilities and his obligations.

The increased inaccurate understanding of abilities for the male partner leads him to behave as though he deserves to be the dominant partner, escalating the degree of inequality between them and causing him to expect acquiescent behavior from the woman.

Practicing Interference Techniques

- Challenging his source of knowledge and seeking the opinions of recognized outside experts—such as bankers, accountants, doctors, mechanics, TV repairers, travel agents, real estate brokers, etc.—can help to reduce the degree of awarding expertise to one's partner where there is no legitimization.
- In addition to increasing her own information, the abdicator will gain a greater respect for her own abilities and decision-making skills.

12. Recognizing Abdicating Behavior: Lack of realistic sense of self-history

An inability to recognize past accomplishments, actions, and activities as worthwhile and adult. The abdicator who relinquishes an understanding of her abilities does not recognize the extent to which her own past work efforts lent support to the unit.

Understanding the Impact

There are two impacts resulting from a behavioral inability to recognize past accomplishments and performance. Both actions and emotions become suspect for the woman who lacks an accurate self-picture.

With respect to action, the impact is to limit self-growth and potential. In regard to emotions, it sets in gear the need to have others define who you are and to give or withhold approval.

The woman then requires an authority figure to

confirm the direction she has chosen or to choose a direction for her.

Practicing Interference Techniques

Phase I
- Begin by making a list of your past accomplishments. List them all.
- Don't disregard those you were not compensated for. If you disregard them, you will not be able to see that you have options and alternatives open to you.
- Do not view accomplishments as stopgap measures. As stopgap measures, accomplishments are not perceived as real or as an important part of your abilities.
- Once you start the process of having to prove yourself over and over again, your capabilities, your intellect, and your ability to both give and receive comfort become crippled.
- As you prepare your list, include household management, jobs and positions that you held prior to and during the relationship, from baby-sitting to summer jobs to full-time positions, and hobbies, interests, and volunteer work you followed through on.
- Think about your assessment of how you performed.
- Take your time—you are listing significant self-enhancing events in your autobiography.
- Don't cheat and don't embellish.

Phase II
- Now begin a list that includes all the positive comments, praise, and compliments that you received from family, friends, work associates. Do not discount these! Praise from any source is significant!

- There is no need for you to list negative comments. If you have practiced abdicating behavior, you have already had sufficient experience to fully integrate them into both your intellectual and emotional sense of self.

Phase III
- Now review your activities and accomplishments for special skills such as organizational ability, writing skills, problem-solving and analytical skills, accounting and human relations skills, etc.
- Circle those activities that represent these skills and others.
- Highlight those actions and traits that represent responsibility, authority, and trust accorded you.

Phase IV
- Now review the lists that you prepared and make notations about the feelings and emotional content you experienced at the time you were engaged in the activities and work efforts listed.
- Make notations about the feelings and emotional content you experienced regarding the comments you received from others about your accomplishments and performance.
- This last phase is the most difficult. You are reviewing your past emotional history and reassessing your present attitudes about yourself.
- Again take your time.
- Don't cheat and don't embellish.

For the woman who lacks a pragmatic sense of self, this technique is as important to her health as a regular medical checkup.

13. Recognizing Abdicating Behavior: De-escalation of expressed needs, wants, and desires

The practice of this behavior erodes the very basis upon which the relationship was built.

Understanding the Impact

The primary impact of settling for less than what you had expected at the beginning of the love relationship is the setting up of a nonnegotiable life-style.

At this point you have the following choices:

- You can decide to break the self-denial pathway and attempt to gain equality by using the interference techniques suggested.
- You can choose to terminate the relationship, which, given your abdicating pattern of behavior, will probably require an outside authority or an escalation of conflict before the termination can be acted upon.
- You can continue in a situation that does not meet your needs.

Practicing Interference Techniques

- Implement and maintain a *monthly needs-wants ledger*. It is often difficult to recognize that we need to make a choice to improve the quality of our lives. Choices will inevitably mean change, and self-initiated change can cause confusion and anxiety. As we undertake the process of deciding whether or not change is warranted, we cannot help but move back and forth from emotional perspective to a pragmatic perspective.
- For many women, particularly those who have practiced abdicating behaviors, the swings from emotional response to pragmatic understanding can create a limbo, a place where we are bound by the inertia of introspection and where action does not seem possible. The primary reason for this inertia is that the emotional content takes precedence over our pragmatic realization of our situation. In this limbo, we

absolutely require documentation of where the relationship is in a practical sense. A needs-wants ledger can provide that documentation and thus prevent us from having to rethink over and over again our reasons for wanting a change.

- Begin your needs-wants ledger by making a list of everything you require within a love relationship. Include sexual fulfillment, security, emotional support, personal freedom, comfort, companionship, affection, and shared activities. Add to the list according to your unique situation.
- Take care not to include items because they appear to be what other people would want from a relationship.
- Once you have your list, check off what you have received during your relationship and what has been lacking.
- Confront your partner with your list, and discuss it openly and honestly.
- Keep a tally, an accounting, of the degree to which your needs are being met for a given period of time. One to three months should allow sufficient time for you to understand and recognize on a pragmatic level how and to what degree your needs are being met. Once the information has been collected and the debits and assets of your relationship have been tallied, you are ready to make your choice. If the assets overrun the debits, you can choose to practice interference techniques to overcome the debits. If the debits overrun the assets, you can choose to continue in a situation that at the most allows you to live with an economy of pain or you can initiate a change that will permit you to maximize your joy. The choice is yours!

Chapter Six

Bitches and Their Lovers

Abdicators fall in love, bitches have lovers.

There are several differences between being in love and having lovers, and the most important one is that being in love is a state of mind, while having a lover is a state of being. In a state of being, there is no sacrifice and there is no compromise.

Sacrifice and compromise and the despair that result form the definition of love for the abdicator:

> Love is defined as a disease for which there is no cure and as a threat to one's life: "If he doesn't call me I'll die." "When I'm not with him I feel sick." Love is perceived in terms of cautions, restrictions, and obligations: "I feel as if I'm walking on eggs when he's around, that I can't be myself, that I have to be what he wants me to be." "I'm afraid of him."

When a woman does not have an understanding of her self-worth, has a poor self-image, and has continuously downgraded her needs, wants, and desires, that is how she defines love.

For bitches and their lovers, there is a different definition:

> Love is defined in terms of the *actions* and *behaviors* displayed by each of the partners to one another. If she defines affection as kissing in the supermarket—that's how he behaves. If he defines comfort as a phone call every night when she's out of town—that's what she does. If she defines nurturing as his playing devil's advocate for her next board meeting—that's the role he takes. If he defines freedom as a weekend alone—that's the freedom she offers. If she defines support as their both sharing equally in household and child rearing chores—that's the contract he makes. If he defines companionship as watching the Superbowl together—that's what they do. If she defines security as a separate bank account—that's what he agrees to. And together they define the commitment, depth, and joy of their love.

This definition not only allows but fosters the magic moments that sharing and equality imply. Both the magic moments *and* the definition need to be shared by both partners in order for love to find concrete reality in a lover.

As women move toward equality in the love relationship, they are subjected to a new set of scenarios within which they define themselves, set up boundaries for their actions, maximize the freedom within those boundaries, and gain acceptance for their behaviors.

Are any of the following speeches familiar to you?

"You need to learn to organize yourself better," he cautions, "so that you can be free (from your job, from your volunteer work, from the children) and be with me when I need you."

"Keep the kids out of here! Can't you see that I'm (working, reading, thinking, watching the game)."

"What do you mean you are going back to school? You

have your bachelor's degree and all you did was secretarial work while I went to law school."

"What do you mean you're going out of town with your boss? Who's going to watch the kids?"

"What do you mean you're running for mayor? Who's going to take care of the house?"

These orders to organize around one partner's needs, demands to protect one partner from the offspring of both, and "What do you means" would not have supported a Geraldine Ferraro, would not have nurtured a Diane Feinstein, would not have encouraged a Margaret Thatcher, and would not have been a demonstration of love to a Barbra Streisand.

Support, nurturance, encouragement, and love do *not* limit. And all of these classical scenarios have the same basic bottom line. *They set up limits to behaviors and activities.*

When abdicator turns bitch and refuses to accept these limits, she becomes involved in activities that are independent of her partner. As she moves towards self-determination, she finds a better job, goes back to school, or becomes an active participant in community organizations instead of a passive recipient of their benefits. Husband and lover often perceive this independence as withdrawal from the relationship rather than a search for self-determination, and when they do, their responses are such that they interfere with the actions chosen by their partners. So let's look at the behaviors used by women to prevent this interference. First, there's Julie.

Julie: "I told my husband that I was going to leave my present job, take a part-time job, and continue graduate school and get my doctorate. In order to do that— continue school—I needed a job that required little initiative on my part, one I could do with little thought but that would bring in at least some of the income that I had been getting from my full-time job. I wasn't putting the entire burden on my husband, just giving him his share. I had been supporting him through graduate school for ten years. He didn't complete it. It was my turn now. I told him that I didn't care whether he agreed with me or not, but I wanted him there for support and to help me as I had helped him. We were sitting in our car, and I said that I didn't see anyone out there holding up signs saying 'I want to support Julie's husband.' I told him if he didn't get a job, then he wouldn't be living with me. It's not that I didn't love him, I do, and I did when I said it, but I wanted a partner and I wanted him to help me. I wanted him to go along with me. He said that he did feel a little different, that he was sure I would do what I set out to do, but he wasn't sure I was making the right decision or the right choices. I said how could he know; the choices were mine, not his. Well, my husband got a job, and in fact, it launched him in his career. He loves it. We're partners, lovers, friends. We support each other. It was a risk, but it was a risk based on a lot of soul-searching about what I wanted, where I was going, and where we were going together."

Julie's behavior was to seek acceptance not agreement and to follow an option of her own selection, not her husband's. She did not equate loving her husband with following his choice.

Women who opted for self-determined behavior within the love relationship experienced significant gains in terms of needs met, respect given, and situational change. More important, they developed an increased realization of self-worth.

Diane's experience with her married lover of five years is a poignant story of such a realization. I began interviewing Diane while she was still in the process of confronting her situation. She had decided that the relationship was deadlocked and that it was time for both of them to make choices. Shortly after she explained her decision to her lover, he decided that he would not separate from his wife. Three weeks after he made that decision he called her, expressed his love for her, and asked to see her again. She refused and said that the choice had been made and that, although she missed him terribly, to see him again would be going back to square one and beginning again the fantasy they had been living for the past five years.

> *Diane:* "When I refused to see him after he called, I felt so free. I finally realized that I'd been a second-stringer because that was how I had set myself up. Now I feel that I'm bright, attractive, desirable, and responsible. I feel that I am an elegant woman. If he makes the decision to separate from his wife and get a divorce, perhaps we'll get together. If not, I'm sure that I will have a relationship with someone else that will be satisfying. Why not? I'm a good catch. For five years I had locked myself in a room with open doors."

The change in Diane's self-image was evidenced by a needed loss of weight, the care she began devoting to her apartment, and her increased energy at work. She looked more lively and more interesting. She was warmer and more concerned with others, and she acted out the role that she said she felt: that of an elegant woman.

For Joann, who had dissolved a twenty-year marriage, the increase in her estimate of self-worth came later.

> *Joann:* "I had to experience success before I could recognize an increase in my self-image. I bought a house. I had a feature article written about me. I won awards in my work. It took accomplishments to increase my self-image. It was the result of doing things on my own, and it took a period of time to find out that I could do it. I was doing the same things during my marriage, but I was limiting myself at the time. My husband's habitual put-down of my

accomplishments and his view of my work as a hobby inhibited my own sense of accomplishment."

After dissolving a fifteen-year marriage, raising three children, and working her way back up to the top of her profession, Barbara, at age forty-seven, has the following definition of romance.

Barbara: "I'm in a very satisfying relationship now. The man I'm dating is younger than I am by nine years, yet our experience, upbringing, and what we want seem to be much the same. I don't want the romance to stop, and by romance I mean that when he is late, I want him to call me; when we disagree, I expect him to listen to me; if I say that I'd like to go sailing, I expect him to join me and not act like he's doing me a favor. That's what romance is: having the other person act with concern, consideration, and respect for what you want and for your ideas."

Concern, consideration, and respect given on a quid pro quo basis were Jennifer's expectations when she entered her first marriage. Jennifer, thirty-eight years old, works as an independent broker planning benefits and compensation for major companies. Her income varies from $40,000 to $60,000 per year. She has been married twice. The first time, she put her husband through school and dissolved the marriage after realizing that he was not going to make any effort toward their comforts or support.

Jennifer: "I divorced him because I was the one doing all the housework, working full time, taking courses at night, while he couldn't do anything but go to school. He was a child, and for a while I treated him as a mother would. He would get upset about a coming exam, and I would hold him and comfort him until three in the morning and go to work. He could sleep late because he had classes that didn't start until the afternoon."

Jennifer continued her story and explained her reasons for marrying and her reassessment of those reasons and her husband's behavior.

Jennifer: "I realized that he needed me, and I felt that I was loved because I was needed. After a while I became tired of fulfilling his needs and not having mine met. I waited until he finished his degree because I felt his behavior would change. I wanted to give our marriage a chance. But he didn't change.

"I remember the incident that made me lose it, just lose my control. I was cooking dinner and reading a magazine. I put the magazine down and went to turn the steak. He came into the kitchen and picked the magazine up and was walking out of the room with it. I told him to leave it because I was reading. He said I wasn't reading, I was cooking dinner. I became furious. I said something that I knew would infuriate him. We had a terrible fight, and the next morning I packed my bags and left. I thought when we got into the process of the divorce that we would separate our assets on an equal basis. I left with $100 in my pocket. He took the rest.

"He called my parents and told them I was a terrible wife. I hadn't been. I supported him both financially and emotionally, and he gave nothing in return. Two years was quite enough to figure that out. I only waited for another two years, until after he got the degree, because I wanted to be fair. When we had gotten married, I had agreed to help support him through his education. Taking the magazine and caring nothing for my needs, for what I wanted, and for what I was, was the final argument."

Rather than wait for twenty years to see if he would change or forget that she was supporting them both and was perfectly capable of supporting herself, Jennifer divorced her husband after four years. She did not excuse her husband's behavior nor did she accept it. She did not believe that there were things she could do and things he couldn't do. She believed and expected that they would share equally in both giving support and receiving comfort.

Jennifer: "I was terrified about my feelings when I decided to leave, terrified because I had _no_ feelings for him. I didn't feel anger or hate; it was just indifference.

"Even if you have a roommate, you have feelings. That was the beginning of my feeling that I was a bitch. I remember my mother saying I was such a cold fish and I had no feelings, but I decided that if that's what I had to do to survive, then I would do it.

"It was scary to think of having lived with someone that long and having zero feeling. In retrospect, I realized that he had changed my love for him. It was his lack of caring that took away my love for him.

"I sacrificed my relationship with my second husband for my career. Before I got married, I wasn't sure that I could support myself. I didn't feel that I had any economic power. By the time we were married, I was making more money than he was. I realized that I could care for myself, and that made me feisty. My husband saw this and began to try to make me back away from my career. The more he did that, the angrier I became and the more I worked at my career. I tripled my salary in a very short time. I was intrigued with my abilities at work.

"He finally gave me an ultimatum to be home at 4:30 P.M. at least twice a week, and I did for a while. But he put subtle pressure on me. He was supportive in front of other people and then would pressure me behind the scenes with little things. When we went to buy a house, I was making more than he was, and he said kiddingly, 'Don't put that down.' He was joking but he meant it.

"He told me that I would have to make a choice between him and my career; not that I would have to stop working but that I would have to take a job that let me be home more. I told him I couldn't make that choice because if I chose him I would be angry with him and destroy us both. We might have made it if he had been more patient and I had been less intrigued with my success. I do want to get married again because I want to share my life and the pleasures that I have with someone I care for. But I want him to care for me in the way that I define caring."

Although Jennifer sacrificed her second marriage to her career, she did it with an understanding and full awareness of how she would feel had she let her husband choose for her what her work life should be. Rather than let the anger build and finally "destroy them both," she followed her own choice. She was well in touch with her feelings and with her husband's. She recognized that he was only giving lip service to her success, and she heard him and the meanings behind his "kidding on the square."

At thirty-five, a continued successful career brought her well-deserved financial security, and Jennifer made a decision that challenged existing social norms to a far greater degree than did her two divorces. She chose to have a child without the sanction of marriage. Now, three years later, her obvious delight with her daughter and the ease with which she has meshed parenting and career testify to the correctness for Jennifer of the creation of this particular life-style.

Jennifer's story bears a closer look. Women who have abdicated and denied themselves the chance to have their needs, wants, and desires met in a love relationship can benefit by asking themselves the following questions about her experience.

- Were her two marriages failures or were they part of a growing process?
- Should Jennifer have abdicated her right in her first marriage to equality of support and caring, as Joann did and as Evelyn did, and toughed it out for twenty years?

- Should Jennifer have abdicated her right in her second marriage to pursue a career, as Gloria did and as Elaine pretended to do, and remain in a marriage for fifteen years?
- Should Jennifer have entered a third marriage with a man whose behavior did not mesh with her needs?
- Should Jennifer have denied herself the right to bear a child because she did not have the sanction of marriage?

Many people would judge Jennifer's behavior as wrong. Some would call it immoral to have a child without the sanction of marriage. Others would call her a bitch for insisting on having an equal measure of support from her lovers, following her potential with her career, and choosing her way with her life.

Some of us would applaud Jennifer's choices to live her life as fully as possible. Some of us would applaud her for creating for herself an alternative life-style that gave her satisfaction, even though it was outside of conventional behavior. Some of us would applaud her courage to dissolve two marriages in spite of how terrified she was about her feelings of indifference toward her first husband after four years of marriage and in the face of her recognition that she was sacrificing her second marriage to her career. Some of us would applaud her for her willingness to enter into another marriage so that she could "share my life and the pleasures that I have with someone that I care for and who cares for me in the way that I define caring."

It is up to you to determine how you would define Jennifer's behavior. Remember, however you would judge and choose for Jennifer, you would also judge and choose for yourself.

An entirely new set of behaviors is practiced within love relationships when the woman begins to disregard the pejorative labels of non-nurturing, overly aggressive, and bitchy. She recognizes the limits that have been placed on her and works to remove them, and she works for acceptance not agreement. She actively seeks her own fulfillment rather than burden her partner by living vicariously through him. She is pragmatic and with her partner seeks to understand the consequences that her behavior might have on their relationship and their love.

All of these actions require a rethinking of old definitions of needs. Barbara redefined romance and translated it into consideration and courtesy from her lover. Jennifer redefined caring and translated it into the kind of behavior that meets her definition of caring and loving. Elaine and Evelyn began to rethink old definitions as they acted out new behaviors.

Elaine: "When I was married, security meant that he liked me, that he showed me affection, that he approved of me, that he would support what I wanted to do. Security meant something that would be given to me. After I completed graduate school and was teaching, security was simply meeting financial needs and nothing more, and financial support is something I can supply, provide for myself, just as I was doing when I supported us both through school."

Evelyn: "If I were to marry again or set up housekeeping, I would give out a test to see how he would respond to me and to what I wanted. I would be on the lookout for a number of things: Was he generous? Would he compromise? Did he remember what I said? How did he speak of other women that he had known? What kind of a relationship did he have with his family? Did he willingly do favors or did he complain about them? There are a number of things I would be looking for, and I would be tempted to keep score. This may sound calculating and nonloving, but it's how I would define an adult relationship. You need to keep sifting the time that you spend together in order to make a judgment of how much time and effort you are going to give to the relationship."

For these women who sought equality over acquiescence within their love relationships, behavioral change preceded the change in their attitudes. Whereas at first they had neglected to set up criteria of expectations within their relationships and had maintained them in spite of unfulfilled needs and dissatisfying situations, these women later, after moving away from or challenging relationships, redefined their needs in terms of the behavior they expected from their partners.

- Love no longer required unconditional agreement; they could still define themselves as loving and disagree with their lovers.
- Security no longer required the maintenance of a dissatisfying relationship; they could provide their own security.
- Support no longer required that they allow their partners to direct their lives in order to be considered deserving; they could make their own choices and still expect respect.

And there are more contrasts between abdicators in love and bitches and their lovers:

- Bitches require equal effort from their lovers; abdicators practice deference.
- Bitches view unrequited love as the stuff of sophomoric romances; the abdicator sacrifices herself for it.
- Bitches view companionship as the sharing of activities they both enjoy; the abdicator plays camp follower to his choice of activities.
- Bitches believe generosity and compromise to be traits expected from both of them; the abdicator relegates these traits to her domain alone.
- Bitches require that affection and friendship be earned; the abdicator offers them unconditionally.
- Bitches demand the freedom to discuss problems; the abdicator circumvents confrontation.

- Bitches understand the need for solitude; the abdicator views it as rejection.
- Bitches recognize independence of social pursuits and work affiliations as the rights of adulthood; the abdicator views them as privileges to be rationed.
- Bitches do not require justification for their behaviors; the abdicator seeks to rationalize.

One of the major behaviors that sets the bitch apart from the abdicator is the ongoing challenging of the relationship.

Dolores recognizes the need to challenge her relationships if she is not to allow herself to settle for less than what she wants. Dolores is forty-seven years old and dissolved a twenty-year marriage that did not meet either her emotional or sexual needs. Her first attempt at divorce was foiled by her husband's heart attack. She withdrew her suit, cared for him during his illness, reconciled with him, and had a second child. Their problems and difficulties remained, and two years after her daughter was born, she obtained a divorce. She discussed the need to assess relationships continuously.

Dolores: "People change. It's as simple as that. I know that at the beginning of a relationship there is a certain amount of waltzing around issues and traits that you see in one another. Some of them you accept and others you don't. Once I see that I'm spending a lot of my time with one person, I begin to confront the behaviors that I don't want. I don't feel that I'm being judgmental or intolerant. I do know that I have a right to surround myself with people who give me pleasure, not people I have to make allowances to myself about.

"Lots of times we start out behaving in one way, and then as things progress, the behavior changes. My expectations are set in motion at the beginning. After all, that's why I started seeing him in the first place. Why should I settle for less just because a period of time has passed? That sounds like I want to be continually courted. I suppose I do, but then I'm willing and I like to court as well. Being sweet and generous and sharing one day a month isn't enough for me. The men I like aren't satisfied with that either."

Assessing a relationship on an ongoing basis requires that we challenge and confront, and conflict is bound to result. Rather than avoid this conflict as the abdicator does, the bitch uses methods that will resolve the conflict once it has surfaced. Some of these methods were born out of trial and error, some of them were consciously planned techniques. Dolores chose to *keep a calendar of events* and discuss them with her lover.

Dolores: "I'm an accountant and a good one. I love my work. I use an accounting method of sorts to make sure that I don't fall into the same trap or habit, thinking it will get better as I did when I was married. I actually wrote a note to myself on a calendar about what happened, whether I was displeased, what bothered me, and what I liked about the time I spent with my lover. My rule is that if I am not writing positive notes at least 75 percent of the time, then I need to talk about what the problem is and get it solved or move on. When I started to keep my calendar, I began to realize that many of the things that bothered me were petty. I was really reacting to other things that had happened at the time, which really had no meaning as far as my lover was concerned. I was also able to get to the things that really bothered me. I showed him my calendar. At first he was furious, and he accused me of keeping accounts on our love. I agreed. I said that's just what I was doing, and since I was good at keeping accounts and since our love was important to me, I would continue to do it. He agreed with me. We didn't fight about it; we just went through the list and came to a compromise that suited the both of us."

Dolores's method of keeping a calendar helped her to avoid several of the behaviors that are practiced by abdicators. First, it prevented her from venting where it's safe and imagining the problem to be solved. Second, it let her know just where she was in terms of receiving satisfaction of her needs. Her calendar would have shown her if she was allowing her lover to take away what was important to her. Third, the problems didn't become habit forming and grow out of proportion because they were allowed to continue. She confronted them within a reasonable time frame and sought to resolve them before continuing with the relationship.

Angela stressed the importance of picking the right time to resolve differences. Angela is forty-three years old, has been married for twenty-two years, and has two children. She is active in the community, serves on several committees, and is an able politician in her own right.

Angela: "When my husband asks me to do something special for him, and then when I do it, he criticizes me or says that I could have done it better, I become furious. But I've learned how to deal with it. He likes pretty nightgowns and has bought me quite a few. One night he mentioned a type that he liked particularly, and the next day I went out and bought one. When I wore it, he said, 'That's nice, but you should have gotten a wrap to go with it.' Here I had gone out of my way and taken time out of a very busy schedule, and he criticized me. I didn't want to bring it up at the time because we were going to make love and, quite frankly, I didn't feel like interrupting my own mood. I waited until he did something similar, and then I brought it up. I asked him how he would feel if he had gone out of his way for me and I criticized him. We talked about it for a while, and he really hadn't thought about the fact that he might be hurting me or putting me down. I found that choosing the right time and getting him to see how it felt to be in the position he had put me in has helped us both resolve the disagreements that we have with one another."

Angela's method of *choosing the right time and the "how would you feel if"* question worked for her. If you choose this method, remember to listen to the answer to your question. If you don't listen, you will be setting up a Ping-Pong match of argument, and rather than settling the disagreement and having your needs met, you will escalate the conflict.

Elizabeth uses a "what's the worst that can happen" method. Elizabeth, at sixty-two, is twice married, the second time for thirty-one years. She has three children and has a lucrative practice as a clinical psychologist.

Elizabeth: "Handling problems is difficult no matter how well trained you are at helping others to solve theirs. Psychologists are no different, and we've had many problems in the past thirty years that have had to be resolved. The barrier to handling conflict is the fear that you have when you attempt to surface the problem. What will happen if I say what I really feel? What will happen if we start to fight? What will happen if I lose? What if he gets me to change my mind?"

There are many "what will happen" questions, and we need to fill in the blanks for ourselves. Had Evelyn, Joann, or other women who practiced abdicating behaviors asked themselves the "what will happen" question, they could very well have gotten on with their lives and taken control of them much sooner than they did.

Gerry's method of resolving conflict was a variation on the accounting method used by Dolores. Gerry is forty-four, has been married for twenty-four years, and has two children. She teaches English in a school in her community.

Gerry: "I'm a writer, a closet writer really, and I've kept a journal since my college days. I've written about lots of the problems that we've had. For several years that's all I did—just write about it. One day I realized that if I didn't publish my writing for my husband as an audience of one, we would be forever fighting and I'd be forever mad at him. I took it out and showed him some of it. Actually, I can't even remember what it was, but that started a different kind of argument for us, with both of us doing the arguing, not just my husband with me listening."

If there is one thread that runs through all of these methods, it is *work*. Keeping a calendar of events, writing about arguments, asking yourself "what if" questions, listening carefully, and choosing the right time all require actively working to seek out methods to resolve conflicts. It is the type of work that requires proactive thinking rather than reactive responding.

Proactive thinking may label you a bitch, but it will bring you equality within the love relationship. Reactive responding may allow you to avoid conflict, but it will cause you to acquiesce in one of the most important areas of your life.

The choice is yours.

Chapter Seven

Preparing Your Case

If we are going to be put on trial for attempting to take control over our lives, change our situation, and demand equality, then we have to prepare our case with care—and with the appropriate behaviors. For those of us who have practiced abdicating behaviors and settled for less than what we wanted, we can use the experiences of our more self-fulfilled sisters. Reading their stories is not enough. If you truly want to move from acquiescence to equality with your husband or lover, it takes effort and it takes practice.

Here's how to do it:

1. *Avoid clichés.* Search for the clichés that you use repeatedly when you are discussing issues in your relationship—phrases like "We can deal with it later," "That's how I am," and "That's not for me." These phrases and clichés that pop into our conversations tend to keep us away from taking action necessary to deal with problems. And they can be as devastating to your move toward equality as Scarlett's "I'll think about it tomorrow."

2. *Initiate Action.* Is it a job that you want to apply for, an investment you want to make, a community leadership role

98

you want to take, or a new career you want to pursue? What-ever it is that you have been putting off, do it now. We can always make time for things that are important to us, but often we have problems taking the first step. Once you have chosen to act, be sure to follow through. Don't leave it half-finished. See it to completion.

3. *Seek acceptance, not agreement.* It is not necessary that your partner agree with what you want to do. It is necessary, if you are going to continue being partners, that he accept your decision and support you in your efforts.

4. *Ask yourself pragmatic questions.* Here are some simple questions, but the answers can lead to a more enriched qual-ity of life as well as more control over your environment:

- What do I want?
- Where do I want to be in the next two, four, six years?
- What are my skills?
- Do I need to improve my skills, my health, my appear-ance?
- What do I wish that I had done?
- If all my dreams, fantasies, and desires came true, what would my life be like?

5. *Disregard derogatory labels.* Too pushy, overly aggres-sive, ball-breaking, cold and calculating, bitch. These are all labels that are applied to the woman who steps out of the abdicator role and aggressively pushes for equality.

6. *Don't accept excuses.* Here are some of the excuses that we use in order to hide from ourselves and our partners that we are not receiving emotional support, love, and caring according to our needs:

- "He isn't capable of caring for me the way I want him to, but I love him anyway."
- "He has never helped in the kitchen; he wouldn't know how."
- "He isn't comfortable with my friends; he doesn't know how to make small talk."

Making excuses allows the behavior to continue. If he says you are right more than once and continues the behavior, then you have still been put off. Get tired of being right all the time. If you are right, then the behavior should change.

7. *Learn about alternatives.* Death and taxes are sure things. The life-style you have now isn't. It's one you've chosen, happened into, lucked into, want to stay in, or can't wait to change. Go about the business of learning the alternatives.

- Does Sally have greener pastures?
- What is it like to live in the city, the country, Middle America, the East Coast or West Coast?
- What life-styles did the latest magazine article you read describe?
- How does the other half live?

8. *Redefine needs in terms of behavior.* Define your needs in terms of the behavior that you want your partner to express. Then tell him how if he doesn't already know.

- "He loves me." How does he show it? How do you want him to show it?
- "I want security." Security of cash or companionship?
- "I want affection and that means kissing me in the supermarket."

9. *Challenge your relationship.* There are plenty of methods available. Just make sure that you share your information with the one who can do something about it—your partner—not your friends. Remember these techniques for conflict resolution:

- Keep a calendar.
- Ask the "what if" question.
- Choose your time.
- Work at it and balance it as you would your checkbook.

While love is not a checkbook, it's up to you to decide how long and to what degree you are willing to be out of balance with your needs, wants, and desires. If fifteen years is too long for you—how about five, or one? And if one year is too short a time for you to determine that your relationship is not one that will ultimately satisfy you, how about two years?

Love stories and happy endings are wonderful, and we have it in our power to write our own. Love stories and happy endings, like most things worth having, require planning, organization, careful thought, and a lot of time polishing to make them just so.

The only way to start is to start taking control.

PART TWO

Parenting

Chapter Eight

Children–Choices
–and Changes

No one would question that equality is a better choice than acquiescence in love relationships or that authority is a better choice than compliance in the world of work. But when it comes to parenting, just what equality is, is hard to define.

Is it abdication to work full time as soon as you're able after childbirth—which for most of us is no longer than four weeks—and leave your child to a nanny, day-care center, relative, or that rarity, the house husband?

Is it abdication to put off having children until your career is in place?

Is it abdication to deny your "womanly function" forever and decide not to ever have children?

Is it abdication to choose to have children without sanction of marriage, without the support of a spouse, without the nurturing of a father?

Let's look at some comparisons and start answering these questions.

The men of the eighties are not abdicators as parents because they work. They become abdicators when they come home from work and demand that their children be whisked away and that someone else give them care and attention.

And women of the eighties who work outside the home are not abdicators as parents because they turn over some of the tasks of child rearing to house husbands, day-care centers, and baby-sitters. They are abdicators only insofar as they do not deliver equal energy to the parenting task.

Careerism, life-style changes, the dissolution of a marriage, and the taking on of another spouse or lover do not cause women to become abdicators as parents. *The degree to which we allow our choices to interfere with the energy, thought, and effort we deliver to child rearing causes us to become abdicators as parents.*

How about delaying childbirth, choosing to have children as a single parent, or deciding against having children altogether? What's the abdicator quotient in these actions? *It's zero.* Why is it that when alternatives and options are finally opened to women, we question whether they should be allowed those options in the first place, instead of thinking about how they can best make use of them? While that's a question that needs to be kept in the forefront, I don't like answering questions with questions.

So specifically—on delaying childbirth—though the statistics are not all in yet, it appears that women who delay childbirth may be giving child rearing tasks more thought and energy than did their predecessors.

And on choosing to be a single parent: choice is precisely the issue here. Many of us have become single parents for a reason other than choice, so to think of ourselves as abdicators when we initiate our status as single parents rather than have it thrust upon us implies that we are less than adult, less than capable, and less than deserving of determining our own life situations. Here, considering the question is characteristic of the thinking of the abdicator. The action of choosing to be a single parent is not abdicator action at all.

And on choosing not to have children at all: once again, that's our choice. Is it possible that when we look at a man who has no children we simply accept it, but when we look at a woman who has no children we become suspicious of her sexuality or motivation, or wonder about her biological ability to have them?

Many of the choices we will make are a function of restrictive self-images and of the supposed to's and ought to's we have believed for so long a time, for example, the single parent who denies herself sex because it doesn't fit her "good mother" image. Or the woman as half of the parenting team in an intact marriage who saves discipline and higher order decisions for her husband. If you are dealing with this question, are you abdicating or have you selectively given some of your power as a parent to your child's father? The answer to the question depends on your belief system and where you place your power base. If you believe that you both are equal parents and if your power base is internal, then you will have no problem about selectively giving some of your parental power to your child's father. If you believe that women should be parents first and adults who have concerns about a number of areas second, and your power base is dependent on your power over your children, then you will not be able to tolerate the give-and-take between your child and your husband. And if, in addition, you work away from home, you have a real problem.

Restrictive self-images and old-hat supposed to's and ought to's cause guilt. They also prevent you from offering your child's father some of the nurturing responsibilities and privileges you may think are yours alone. Denying the father these privileges and responsibilities does not make you a more effective parent; it only serves to limit your choices. And limiting choices can cause abdication.

We become abdicators as parents when we are neither caring nor concerned. How do we assess caring versus noncaring in terms of the behavior that we see? How do we assess concern versus lack of concern in terms of the actions as parents we take toward our children? We need a starting place. For me that starting place is what children deserve, what they should be permitted to do, and what they should be allowed to become.

Chapter Nine

Children: Equal Time

He held me up over his head against the wall. He was tall enough so that my head reached the ceiling. He kept banging me against the wall, shouting to my stepmother, "Is this what you want? Is this what you want?" I was about four years old.

I have acne and he used to say, "I've seen better skin on whores in the street." I was twelve then.

The will read: "And to my daughter, for reasons best known to herself, I leave nothing." I was thirty-seven years old when he died.

The experiences you have just read about were mine. They form a crucial portion of my background. The reader has a right to know what motivated me and how I've come to feel so strongly about what I *insist* children deserve.

I have two sons. Jason is eighteen and Russell is fourteen. I have raised them as a single parent for the past twelve years—

though not without sincere concern and reliable support from their father. My beliefs about child rearing leave no room for ambiguity.

Here they are:

- Children deserve unconditional love, unconditional support, and unconditional affection. And children deserve this from the second that they are born, not only when they begin to rebel.
- Children deserve the same degree of energy from us that we give to our work, to our play, to our running, to our handball, to our lovemaking. And children deserve to know that this is an energy born of joy not duty, of pleasure not obligation, and of love for *them,* not from fear that they won't love *us.*
- Children deserve honesty, as we share with them our successes and most especially as we share our failures. Children deserve this because we must pave the way for what really happens in life and not play super star to their ordinary and unique, average and miraculous selves.
- Children deserve to be offered reality that is monitored by their own ability to accept it and not by our own needs for emotional release.
- Children deserve to be fed responsibility in as careful doses as we wean them from the breast to formula, to rice cereal and bananas, to peaches and broccoli and meats, and finally to caviar, artichokes, escargot, and sushi. At each new taste, children deserve to choose the level of responsibility they are both capable of and willing to handle.
- Children deserve to revel in self-pride and to relish their vanity. They deserve this because when pride precedes failure it provides a healthy cushion.
- Children deserve to be lavished with fun, joy, jokes, laughter, happy times. Children deserve this ritual of joy on a daily basis with breakfast, lunch, and dinner

because it allows them to develop their own personal antibodies to failure, disappointment, depression, anxiety, and all those other forms of emotional pain.

- Children deserve to be protected as they travel from infancy to preadolescence to adolescence to adulthood. They deserve this because it's hard, difficult, dangerous, and scary to move from one stage to another. As their parents, we are permitted to shelter their souls and spirits from bruises just as we allow ourselves to soothe their bodies.

- Children deserve to know that they don't interfere with us, they interact with us; that they don't need to live up to our expectations but may set their own; that no matter what we do they are our best products.

- Children deserve powerful positive memories to protect them when we die.

These are the things that I believe children deserve. Don't let my own personal history and the litany that results hamper you. Add to your own list. Though it will be based on your own unique history, whether loving or not, the privilege of parenthood permits us to change history as we transmit it. The direction of the change is determined by what we did or did not receive of our just deserts as children.

If your childhood balance sheet is in the red, then, as I did, you will have to go through a grieving process for that small person you once were. A grieving process that allows you to shed tears freely for having been denied. Not so easy—this sorrow. After all, we're adults now, and we've been told that adults shouldn't feel sorry for themselves. What behaviors teach our children to withhold and to hide from themselves their personal sorrows?

The abdicator practices them well as she relies on shoulds or ought to's and supposed to's that come from a superficial understanding of the needs of her children and of the actions she must take to meet them. The bitch confronts the sorrows of her children and helps them grow through them.

Not only is this sorrow hard to come by in terms of what we are permitted to feel, but because it is a sorrow for who we once were, it is hard for us to believe that we still deserve our grief. We are no longer innocent. After all, look at all the mistakes we've made, the betrayals we've practiced, how we've modified, adjusted, compromised, rationalized, put off decisions. Do we still deserve that sorrow? You bet your life we do! And we lose essential ingredients of living—self-forgiveness, risk taking, contentment, and joy—if we don't.

What behaviors teach our children that only the perfect, the ideal, the socially determined good guys deserve our grief or sympathy? Where does that place the rest of us? The abdicator reserves the rights of deserving for "show and tell" children. The bitch's children are deserving because they *are*.

What should children be permitted? This is what children should be permitted:

- Children should be permitted to cry for needs that go unsatisfied. They should be permitted to learn that after tears comes planning, so that the next time—and there is always a next time—they will be better able to meet their needs.

- Children should be permitted to spill their milk, lose their gloves, and lose their lunch money because these things represent superficial belongings; anger over their loss replaces what should be a daily ritual of loving.

- Children should be permitted to play out their fantasies without ridicule, to understand that it is all right to know more than we do and that it is perfectly fine to not know as much.

- Children should be permitted to question us and not understand our answers the first, second, or third time around; to challenge us and receive careful responses, not reprisal; to build their own value systems and not fear their conflict with ours.

- Children should be permitted to be inconsistent as they take responsibility and then relinquish it; as they assume maturity and then retrace the childish behaviors of a previous passage, and as they ask for freedom and then rail at us for giving it.

- Children should be permitted to see us take their sides in the public view and hear our lectures, exhortations, and frustrations over their behavior—not over *them*—not ever over *them*—in private.
- Children should be permitted to become whatever they will become within the space they live in; children should be safe, secure, and well tended by parents who do not abdicate their parenthood.

What should children be allowed to become? This is what children should be allowed to become:

- Children should be allowed to become good students and bad ones; to become draft dodgers and marines; to become mechanics and college students; to become housewives and career women. Just as we allowed ourselves to become.
- Children should be allowed to become people who forgive themselves their mistakes so that they don't become plastic, frozen, frightened people.
- Children should be allowed to become people who judge themselves according to their own measuring stick but do not judge others by it.
- Children should be allowed to become people who take risks in loving and in their livelihoods, monitoring those risks against their experiences and through honest discussions of the experiences of their parents.
- Children should be allowed to become people who accept their limits, whether they strive to go beyond them or not.
- Children should be allowed to become people who will be able to take preventive measures against their obstacles rather than meet them unawares as a new crisis each time.

● Children should be allowed to become people who seek joy, not avoid it; who distribute joy, not withhold it; who maintain joy, not lose it.

The abdicator does not *allow* children; she disavows them. She is embarrassed by them and so she hides them—even from herself. She apologizes for them when there is no need and praises them when there is no cause. The bitch guides her children, sets their boundaries, and with care, caution, and concern, slowly relaxes the limits as she hands over the reins for *becoming*.

Child abuse comes in many forms. The abdicator who relinquishes her parenthood, displays ambivalence, focuses on the superficial, hands her authority over to institutions, and plays the "Don't blame me if you get into trouble" game is well practiced in the hurtful art of covert child abuse manifested through ambiguous behaviors.

Come now and meet the abdicator as she relinquishes her parenthood to spouse and lover, to professionals and institutions—and to her sons and daughters—as she plays the role of the mythical mother.

Chapter Ten

The Abdicator as Mythical Mother

Sad Stories from Sour Grapes

The abdicator as mythical mother transmits history without improving it. Either because she's forgotten or because she did not grieve sufficiently through her own denial of her past or because she does not devote to parenting the energy it deserves, the history she provides her children with becomes self-serving instead of mutually nurturing.

The self-serving nature of her behavior is reflected in easy-way-out choices in her interactions with her children. In place of explanations, she issues orders. In place of in-depth communication, she offers platitudes. In place of developing her children's emotional health, she chooses to focus on the superficial. The loss is hers and her children's. As her children fail to gain the security, love, and comfort they need, she fails to gain the satisfaction of meeting those needs.

Whether the abdicator is parenting as a single parent or as half of the parenting team, the issue is not why she abdicates or what her intentions were. The concern is *how* she abdicates

114

and the impact her behavior has on her children and herself. Whether active or passive in her methods, what she abdicates and relinquishes control over is the delivery of what children deserve, the permission that is their right, and the freedom to become themselves rather than replicas of what their parents are or models of what they could not be.

Wearing the banner of her culturally awarded authority as a parent, Marcia's mother, Marion J., exemplifies the woman who actively withholds the rights of childhood from her children as she attempts to relive her own. In place of those rights, she serves uneasiness, anxiety, and a fear that is not so easily recognized and thus not readily exorcised.

> *Marcia:* "When I was a kid, we used to call home. Me, my brother Tom, and my sister Christy. The first thing we would ask is 'What kind of mood is Mother in?' You know, to find out if you wanted to come home right then or if you should stay at your friend's house for another hour and hope that Mother's mood might change. You never knew what was bothering her. You would walk into the living room and Mother would be sitting on the couch with her face stretched out, and you would say, 'What's wrong, Mother?' Nothing. Just dead silence. 'What's wrong, Mother?' Sometimes she would come out with it and then it was everything. She'd say, 'Nothing goes right around here. Nobody does anything around here.' You know, like everything was falling apart. Most of the time she would say nothing. It seemed that if you didn't know what was bothering her, then you didn't love her."

What kind of a home was it that Marcia, Tom, and Christy were afraid to come home to? *It was a home where the children were expected to intuit needs rather than have them explained.* The game is called, Guess what's bothering me today? The role given the children is that of frantic searchers after phantom problems. Since their search is neverending and bound to fail, they are programmed to become adults who either forego pleasing behaviors, since they have learned that they beget no positive results, or they become pleasers who lose touch with themselves and with their own needs, wants, and desires.

The game is usually played during the first major interaction of the day, when the child returns from school or when the parent returns from work. As such, the game becomes the child's daily welcome-home ritual. And it is abusive.

As adults we have both used and heard the remark, "I need time to put my work, my day, behind me before I can join the family again." We come home and shed our office uniform, check the mail, the *TV Guide,* the refrigerator, and the stove. And then—only then—are we ready to join in, listen, and be listened to.

Children require the same space. They don't usually have any mail to handle, and the stove and refrigerator are approached as functional requirements only and not as an escape hatch. In fact, they have not yet learned that they *need* an escape hatch or that one might be available.

Marion J.'s children had no escape hatch. Instead of being welcomed to a space that was safe, secure, and well tended by parents who did not abdicate their parenthood, their welcome mat was anxiety. The home that they were afraid to come back to was, according to her eldest daughter, a home that "was reigned over by a woman who was caught in the time warp where women had to choose between career and family. Mother was Phi Beta Kappa and had been accepted to law school, but she chose to help Daddy up the corporate ladder instead."

If Marion J.'s goal was her husband's success, then we can assume it was achieved. Marcia's father was president of a Fortune 500 firm and commanded a six-figure income from the mid-1960s until he retired in 1980. If her goal was parenting, she chose to meet it with *negative prophecies,* rather than channel her considerable abilities and energy into mature and thoughtful child-rearing behavior.

Marcia: Mother was always projecting tremendous disaster. I'll never forget the time when I was going into the ninth grade. I had to take a biology course. One day I walked into the living room, and my mother was sitting on the couch and crying. And I said, 'Why are you crying, Mother?' And she said, 'Because I know you're going to flunk biology.' This was in September before school had even started. I said, 'Why do you think I'm going to fail?' She said, 'Because you do very badly in math and science and I just know you'll flunk biology.'

"We used to walk into Woolworth's, and there would be a very ugly, very humpbacked, overly made up woman with dyed black and thinning hair sitting behind the ribbon counter. And my mother would always point to that woman and say, 'If you don't do well in school that's where you'll end up. This is what you will become.' I still feel anxiety whenever I pass a Woolworth store."

The use of negative prophecy provides the mythical mother with a win-win setup, as it allows her to maintain control over the best of worlds and the worst of worlds. If the child fails, her warning allows her to disclaim ownership and thus relinquish responsibility. If the child succeeds, her caution allows her to perceive herself as instrumental in this accomplishment.

While the practice of negative prophecy allowed Marion J. to be consistently in the right, the double-bind message she offered was *inconsistency*.

Marcia: "All the time I was either pretty or I was ugly, I was either smart or I was dumb, I was either a good kid or a bad kid, I was either a nice kid or a rebellious strong-willed kid. When I made the national honor society, she was happy for twenty-four hours. The next day she said I'd never get into college."

She played the "Guess what's bothering me today?" game and offered her children negative prophecies and inconsistencies, with the skill that only a Phi Beta Kappa can muster.

Marcia: "It was Christmas eve about eight years ago and Mother was going to the early church service. It was five o'clock, and she would be back about seven o'clock. Five is cocktail time at our house, and I said to my father, 'Well, it's five, let's have a drink.' Mother was coming downstairs to put on her lipstick to go over to church. Mother would never have a drink before she went to church. She thought it was improper to show up with liquor on your breath. When she saw Daddy and me make drinks, her face froze and she became sullen. Mother sulks when she's upset. She was in the bathroom with this horrible grimace on her face, peering into the mirror, putting on her lipstick, and I could just sense her anger. So I went to the bathroom, and I said, 'What's wrong, Mother?' 'Nothing is wrong.' And I just couldn't take this shit anymore, so I said, 'For Christ's sake, what are you upset about? I know you're upset about something, and nobody can do a bloody thing for you unless you say what's wrong.' 'You're having cocktails without me. I thought everyone would wait for me to come home before having a drink.' I said, 'Well, Mother, look, the drinks are already made. We'll have one now, we'll wait for you to come home, and then we'll have one at seven.'

"But you see she had it in her head that everyone should wait for her to come home, and my father, my brother, and I would wait. Not because it was wrong to have a drink, not because it was illicit or sinful or she thought that we'd all be drunk, it was simply that we should all wait for her. She would take very small things and she would create a nightmare because she felt slighted."

The needs Marion J. demanded to be filled were of the same quality as those she offered to fill—fringe and superficial. By far the greatest portion of Marion J.'s relationship with her children was the relationship she sought for them within the world of school and grades, of clean clothes and cashmere sweaters, of polite phrases and brief bridge club appearances. *It was a relationship of show-and-tell value.*

The mythical mother who parades her children for their show-and-tell value denigrates their worth within the confines of the family unit, while praising them to the world outside. The crux of the behavior is dishonesty regarding their successes and failures. While the young child might enjoy false praise, as he or she grows older, he or she begins to understand the disparity, with the result that the child disassociates himself or herself from parental authority and trust.

The loss was both to Marion and to her children—the loss of a mutuality of nurturance, comfort, support, and confidence sharing.

In place of teaching responsibility, the mythical mother distributes chores. In place of understanding their interests, she demands grades. In place of teaching respect, she requires good manners. In place of meeting their needs, she seeks to gratify her own. In place of demonstrating unconditional love, she requires that they seek her approval. As she avoids practicing those behaviors through which love is transmitted, she equates her children's behavior with the children themselves, never separating the two from her exhortations nor separating them for her children.

The impact on children can be devastating, because it prevents the development of self-worth and self-confidence. It directly demonstrates to children that parental love is dependent on what they do rather than on who they are, and as they go about the process of choosing their behavioral responses, they measure them against what they believe will gain them the approbation and love that they seek from their parents. When those choices are in conflict with their own unique needs, they are caught in an emotional no-win situation. If the children choose the route to gain parental approval, they lose the satisfaction of their needs. If they choose to satisfy their own needs, they lose the security of parental approval. Since children have learned to view parental love as conditional upon their behavior, they no longer have the family as a safe place within which to test and rehearse their behavior. Children run the risk of becoming adults who are constantly looking over their shoulder for the rejection they have come to expect. Turning this abuse inward, they come to believe the following:

- I am not capable; *not,* I can find a way of learning this.
- I am ugly; *not,* I would look better if I lost ten pounds.
- I am bad; *not,* I should have put the glass on the table instead of on the rug.
- I am not deserving of love; *not,* my mother didn't know how to be loving.

Marion J.'s misuse of her parental authority and her focus on the superficial, coupled with the delivery of negative prophecies, did, indeed, allow her to maintain control. She was able to prevent the worst by disavowing the best. She took control but relinquished responsibility.

The bottom line of relinquishing responsibility for child rearing while maintaining control over situations is the role reversal that results when our children are burdened with our discontent and blamed for our disappointments while we demand that they play mind reader of our needs.

There are other paths to role reversal, as we'll see.

Chapter Eleven

"I Didn't Know It Was Happening"

My daughter is twenty-three. I found out two years ago that her father used to beat her. She told me that once she went to school with bruises and the school authorities came to the house to talk to my husband about it. I never knew about it. I thought he was just spanking her.

As the primary care-taking parent, mothers are often able to pick up on the subclinical cues that our children are not feeling well. We don't wait for them to complain about an earache or run a fever before we recognize that they are coming down with something. And so we do our best to catch the cold before it becomes a sore throat, and we take preventive measures. *We are not always so in tune with the behavioral cues children send us to indicate the coming of emotional pain. We withhold credibility from them because they are "just children," and we disregard the comments and observations of others who suggest that something could be wrong.*

This was the pattern that Valerie's abdicating behavior took in her interactions with her husband and his philosophy of child rearing.

Valerie: "We always had a different philosophy when it came to rearing the children. I believed, perhaps naively, that if you gave them enough love and guidance eventually everything would work out all right. My husband was a strict disciplinarian. He believed in not having any back talk. I believed that they should have a religious background. He thought that religion was a bunch of baloney and told them so. There was always a conflict there. And the children would get different messages from us. I believed then that parents need to decide on the form of discipline they are going to give to their children and then present them with a united front so they didn't get into the habit of trying to play one parent against the other."

The ideological view that there is inherent in the family structure an adversary relationship between parents and children coupled with the implication that somehow our children will be able to manipulate us without our knowledge can lead us to ignore parental behaviors that are potentially harmful or presently dangerous to the child. When we ignore the behaviors, we also ignore the reactions they elicit.

Valerie: "My daughter started to put on weight when she was about to go into puberty. Most children do. Her father called her fatso. And at the dinner table he would talk about the food she shouldn't eat. She shouldn't eat the mashed potatoes or the doughnuts. There were many times when he sent her away from the table. She would rebel and that made things worse. It was about that time that she became overly concerned about her appearance and refused to go out with us on family outings. She changed her friends. She suddenly started to choose friends who were not the popular kids."

Recognizing the behavioral cues that indicate the condition of your child's emotional health requires that you pay attention to body language, verbal behavior, behavioral changes, facial expression, the look in her eyes, and the way she does or does not make eye contact with you.

We all have had plenty of practice recognizing the signs that gives us a sense of the emotional state people are in. We've done it in bars, with people whose attention we wanted, and with those we wanted to ignore. We've done it at work with our bosses, subordinates, and peers. We've done it in bed with our husbands and lovers. And if we don't know how to do it, we read books about it.

For our children, we need to transfer those skills for their benefit as well as for our own. To do less is child abuse.

While her husband was escalating his abuse from name calling to beatings and her daughter was moving from childish pouting to increased rebellion, Valerie was becoming more and more distanced from what was actually happening between her husband and her daughter, her husband and her two sons, and her husband's participation in the family unit as a whole.

The point is that there are times when mothers must act to protect their children from their fathers and when fathers must act to protect their children from their mothers. In order to recognize that protection is necessary, we need to challenge our ideologies and understand the family power structure. When we withhold that protection, we become accessories to child abuse.

Valerie played the role of accessory.

Valerie: "I don't remember saying anything when my husband challenged her about her weight, and I thought he was just sending her to her room and giving her a smack when he was really beating her. The only reason I waited so long to divorce him was that I thought the boys needed his guidance. When I look back at it, and there were enough of my friends at the time who talked to me about it, I can see now that he abandoned his role as a parent. He was gone the whole week and would come in on Fridays screaming at them. Saturday he worked on the yard, and Sunday he worked on a car he was remodeling. Once he took the boys to a car show, but when he got there, he left them to fend for themselves and went off to talk to his friends. That's not parenting, that's abandoning. I had thought that he would pay more attention to their school-work, but all he wanted to know about were the grades. He wasn't interested in what they were doing or what they liked."

Two years after her divorce, Valerie's philosophy of love and guidance opened communication between her and her daughter and enhanced the relationship she had always enjoyed with her sons.

Valerie: "My daughter and I are talking about what she experienced with her father. At first she resisted it and didn't want to tell me. I persisted. I had to know what happened and she had to know why I didn't do anything. Before I knew about it, I had told her that she should try to improve her relationship with her father. Now I don't think she has to and I told her so, and I know that she's relieved."

Persistence and initiation of communication keeps us aware as parents and allows us to make knowledgeable judgments as to the direction our guidance should take.

Valerie: "The boys are adults now. Bruce is twenty-six. He was living with a young woman and I talked to him about it. Bruce is a homebody, and even though he said he'd be content to continue to live with Joyce, I felt it would be better for him if they considered marriage. They did get married, and I can see that he's become more mature. He makes more decisions and he's more motivated than he was. I'm glad we talked about it. Adult or not, I have more experience than they do, and it's one of the more important things I can give them."

Valerie made the transition from mythical mother to nurturing parent when she assumed the caretaker role and took responsibility rather than relinquishing it. In the next chapter, we see the patterns and behaviors of abdication and begin the process of running interference with them.

Chapter Twelve

The Abdicator's Pathway to Weakness

The following diagram of behaviors outlines the abdicator's pathway to weakness, and regardless of the particular combinations of behaviors practiced, the bottom line—role reversal—where parent becomes child, and child is forced to assume the adult role—is the same.

DIAGRAM 2. The Abdicator's Pathway to Weakness

Guess What's Bothering Me Now?

↓

Negative Prophecy

↓

Children for Show and Tell

↓

You Are What Your Behavior Is

↓

Instant Responsibility

↓

Abstract Rules

↓

Unchallenged Ideologies

↓

Ignoring Behavioral Cues

↓

Avoiding Family History

↓

Result: Role Reversal

The Three-Step Process Toward Strength in Parenting

The following section outlines the *Three-Step Process Toward Strength in Parenting* and allows the reader to see at a glance the abdicating behaviors, the impact they have on the child and parent, and the techniques that can be used to interfere with the role reversal that is the result of relinquishing control over child rearing.

We all have made and will make mistakes in child rearing. No matter how concerned and enlightened we are, there will be days, times, and incidents when our behaviors as parents will not be geared to what's best for the child but what's best for us. Just about anything can interfere with the all-engaging task of child rearing. That is precisely the point. Because child rearing is so all-engaging, and because we can't "be there" all the time, it is imperative that our child-rearing techniques, methods, and behaviors be well planned and intentional rather than haphazard and accidental. The three-step process is designed with that in mind. Read the information in the table and then the full explanation that follows.

TABLE 2. THE THREE-STEP PROCESS TOWARD STRENGTH IN PARENTING

Step I: Recognizing Abdicating Behavior	Step II: Understanding the Impact	Step III: Practicing Interference Techniques
1. Guess what's bothering me now?	Causes general and unidentifiable unease Leads to role reversal	• Establish a "welcome home" ritual • Be specific about concerns and problems • Consciously choose time to show concern
2. Negative prophecy	Undermines self-confidence and goal setting Undermines parental trust	• Check out child's interests • Contrast interests with demonstrated skills and abilities • Be sure to get his or her views before you give yours
3. Children for show and tell	Presents double message Causes low self-esteem Leads to mistrust of parental information and authority	• List child's positive and negative traits and the behaviors they are associated with • Set priorities with traits from most important to least important • Review lists with spouse or family members • Plan time to discuss both positive and negative traits with child
4. You are what your behavior is	Prevents development of self-esteem Causes unease and anxiety	• Remove the personal pronoun from your interactions when you challenge his behavior • Discuss the behavior in terms of consequences and benefits • Expect disagreements

Step I: Recognizing Abdicating Behavior	Step II: Understanding the Impact	Step III: Practicing Interference Techniques
5. Instant responsibility	Child mistakes responsibility for chores to be completed. Benefits of assuming responsibility are not learned	• List areas of responsibility and related benefits to child • List chores and benefits to household • Discuss benefits with child
6. Abstract rules	Undermines parental authority	• List house rules and purpose • Share information with child • Compromise on lower order rules
7. Unchallenged ideologies	Leads to misuse of parental authority. Stereotypes individual child. Prevents recognition of possible problem situation with adult community	• Prepare your own litany of what children deserve, should be permitted to do, and should be allowed to become • Compare list with spouse or friend • Write out an explanation and purpose for each point you have listed
8. Ignoring behavioral clues	Leads to crisis intervention as opposed to preventive child care. Prevents recognition of both positive and negative feedback from child	• Review child's behavior over time • Include interaction with family, peers, acquaintances, schoolwork, and outside interests

Step I: Recognizing Abdicating Behavior	Step II: Understanding the Impact	Step III: Practicing Interference Techniques
9. Avoiding family history	Promotes crisis intervention methods Escalates problem Leads to shame and dissembling in family dynamics	• Use role-play methods for younger children • List conflict areas • Compare lists with family members • Set priorities from most to least important conflict

1. Recognizing Abdicating Behavior: Guess what's bothering me now

Expressing displeasure with the individual child, siblings, spouse, or family circumstances while withholding specific reasons for discontent.

Understanding the Impact:

This causes general and unidentifiable unease, discomfort, and insecurity in the child who is the primary target as well as in siblings.

If this is a habitual pattern, family members will usually challenge it with a consistent phrase, i.e., "What's wrong with you now?" "What's bothering you?" Consistent phrasing is a cue to the habitual nature of the message that you are sending and thus alerts you to the need to interfere with it.

Practicing Interference Techniques:

● Establish a "welcome home" ritual. The welcome home ritual can set up the emotional space that the child requires in order to rejoin the family. In addition, since nonspecific displeasure is most often demonstrated during this major daily interaction, the welcome home ritual prevents its occurrence.

- Plan occasional surprises, presents, and outings, and mark dates on the daily calendar you keep for social and business appointments.
- Set up a specific time for each child where concerns, issues, and problems can be discussed.

2. Recognizing Abdicating Behavior: Negative prophecy

Telling the child that she or he will fail at what she or he is at present attempting to accomplish or telling the child that her or his future goals are unlikely to be realized. Setting up extraordinary standards, while simultaneously berating the child for not meeting them. Offering either superstar or below-average examples as role models for goals the child has set for herself or himself.

Understanding the Impact:

This undermines self-confidence and goal setting. It causes children to expend less effort than they are capable of. It undermines sharing of problems, concerns, and issues regardless of origin, i.e., school, social, sibling, or other parent issue.

Practicing Interference Techniques:

- Check out your child's interests.
- Get her or his views before you give your own.
- Contrast her or his interests with the skills and abilities she or he has demonstrated.
- Initiating such a dialogue and starting the process of collecting the information will serve as a trigger to jog your memory and interfere with negativism that you may be practicing.

3. Recognizing Abdicating Behavior: Children for show and tell

Praising the child in front of others while denigrating his or her worth within the confines of the family unit.

Understanding the Impact:
This presents the child with conflicting perceptions of his or her behavior and identity. It causes low self-esteem and mistrust of parental information and authority.

Practicing Interference Techniques:
Since the crux of demonstrating behavior that causes us to use our children for their show-and-tell value is at the least an unrealistic but well-meaning assessment of the children's abilities and at worst a purposefully dishonest presentation of their attributes, techniques designed to interfere with the behavior must permit an objective analysis of the children's strengths and weaknesses. The following four-phase process is designed to surface that objective analysis.

In a two-parent family, have your spouse complete the process with you. In a single-parent family, choose a family member (not a sibling) or close friend to complete the process. Do not compare the lists you develop as you complete the process until you have each completed the first three phases.

Phase I
- List both the positive and negative traits your child exhibits in her or his interactions at school, in social gatherings, and with family members.
- List the priority of those traits from the most important to least important.

Phase II
- For each trait that you have listed, write out an explanation of why you believe that behavior to be either positive or negative.
- Be explicit. An explanation that reads, "Because it's good for him (or her)" won't do.

Phase III
- Exchange lists with your spouse, family member, or friend. Silently read through your partner's lists before you discuss them. Begin your discussion, taking care to keep

it a two-way interaction. Listen carefully to the reasons offered by your partner.

- Don't turn the discussion into a shouting match.
- As you review your two sets of lists, come up with a single set that you both agree on.
- If you find that there are areas where you cannot agree, do not disregard those items. Keep them as part of your combined list.

Phase IV   In this phase you will plan intentional interactions with the children.

- Use your calendar to plan time when you will work on praising the child for the positive traits and discussing with him or her the negative aspects of his or her behavior. Praising positive traits fits well into a "welcome home" ritual. Discussing negative behavior should occur when you or your spouse have separate time with the child, not while engaging in activities that include other family members.
- Do not confront more than one negative aspect at a time.
- Keep your discussion open-ended and be careful to get your child's view before you offer your own.

4. Recognizing Abdicating Behavior: You are what your behavior is

Expressing to the child that you are disappointed in him or her and that you disapprove of him or her, instead of challenging the behavior that he or she has exhibited.

Understanding the Impact:

This prevents the development of self-worth and self-confidence. It demonstrates to the child that your love for him or her is dependent upon what he or she does, not who he or she is. It causes unease and anxiety.

Practicing Interference Techniques:
- Remove the personal pronoun from your interactions with the child when you challenge his or her behavior.
- Discuss the behavior in terms of the consequences it has for the child, allowing him or her to give his or her views of what those consequences might be before you offer your views.
- Discuss the benefits to the child in refraining from that behavior or changing and modifying it.
- Expect disagreements, and expect to spend time and effort in the discussion.

5. Recognizing Abdicating Behavior: Instant responsibility
Handing responsibility to children based upon parent's needs. Expecting full and immediate compliance with responsibilities distributed. Maintaining rigid guidelines within which responsibilities are to be handled by the child.

Understanding the Impact:
The child views responsibilities as chores to be accomplished, as opposed to recognizing the benefits of assuming responsibility and control for personal needs and their gratification.

Practicing Interference Techniques:
The delivery of instant responsibility results when the distinction between chores and responsibility is not clear either from the parent's perspective or the child's. When the requirement to complete chores replaces the teaching of responsibility, the benefit to the child is absent. The following method is designed to insure that there is a distinction made between chores and responsibility and that,

when responsibility is the issue, there is a clear benefit to the child.

- List areas of responsibility and chores that you believe should be assumed or completed by the child.
- Write out the benefit that the child will realize if the area of responsibility is acted upon successfully by the child.
- Write out the benefit to the household that will result if chore completion is accomplished.
- Take time to explain the benefits and consequences of responsibility and chore completion to the child. Get his or her thoughts, regardless of whether or not you choose to share the decision with respect to chores completed or responsibility assumed.

6. Recognizing Abdicating Behavior: Abstract rules
Imposing rules on children without adequate explanation of their rationale or purpose.

Understanding the Impact:
This undermines parental authority. It teaches nonanalytical thinking and unquestioned acceptance of rules, regulations, ought to's, and supposed to's.

Practicing Interference Techniques:
- List house rules and write out rationale for enforcing them.
- Share information with the child, and get her or his views.
- Combine your views and put the rules in order of priority.

7. Recognizing Abdicating Behavior: Unchallenged ideologies
Allowing child-rearing behaviors to be directed by outdated assumptions regarding the parent–child relationship. Adhering to the "I was raised this way and look how well I turned out" philosophy, thus neglecting to improve upon the child-rearing behaviors that you were subjected to.

Understanding the Impact:

The impact of unchallenged ideologies is far-reaching and includes the misuse of parental authority as demonstrated by setting down rules that are based on the abstract, that are untenable in today's society, and that do not take into account the particular and unique behavior of the individual child. Thus, rather than treating the child as unique, the child is stereotyped and treated as a member of a particular group. This leads to the withholding of credibility from the child, thus preventing the parent from understanding the rationale within which the child's behavior is founded. It leads to the inability to challenge behaviors of authority figures, including possible detrimental behaviors of a spouse or educational, medical, or religious professionals who affect the child's growth and development.

Practicing Interference Techniques:

Phase I ● Write out your own litany of what you believe that children deserve, should be permitted to do, and should be allowed to become.

Phase II ● Write out an explanation and purpose for each point you have made.

Phase III ● Enlist the aid of spouse, family member, or friend and compare and discuss list.

The primary benefit of this technique is that it will solidify for you what your beliefs are and on what they are founded. It is helpful to share the list with the child and to refer to it from time to time. After a while, it becomes a part of your habitual parenting style.

8. Recognizing Abdicating Behavior: Ignoring behavioral cues

Lack of attention to changes in child's behavior vis-à-vis her or his relationship to you, the other parent, siblings, peer group, and school, medical, or other authority figures that affect the child.

Understanding the Impact:
This sets us up as parents who are reactive to crisis as opposed to active in preventing difficulties. It allows continuance of behavior and exacerbates it. It prevents us from giving positive feedback or negative feedback.

Practicing Interference Techniques:
- Set up a system comparing the individual child's behavior over time.
- Include such items as interaction with family, peers, and acquaintances and participation and interest in schoolwork and outside activities.
- The system need not be complex. A diary or letter that you write and keep for yourself can suffice.
- Once you have begun the process, it becomes habitual, allowing you to recognize changes as they occur.

9. Recognizing Abdicating Behavior: Avoiding family history

Refusing to recognize areas of conflict between yourself and your child or between the child and spouse, stepparent, members of the extended family, or family friends.

Understanding the Impact:
This allows recognition of a problem only when a crisis has occurred, thus permitting crisis intervention as opposed to preventive measures. It exacerbates the problem by allowing its continuance. Cues that a problem exists will probably have been given by members outside of the family unit, either by school officials and associates or by peer group parents or by members of the extended family.

Practicing Interference Techniques:
- As in all the interference techniques, the first step is recognition. For young children, role playing is a very effective method of understanding their perception of the interaction between themselves and their parents as

well as with other family and extended family members.

- Establish the role: "You play the Mommy or Daddy, sister, grandmother, baby-sitter, and I'll play the baby."
- Then set up the situation—it is dinner time or bedtime or pretend to engage in activities that are both praised and challenged by the adult figure.
- In this instance, the child's perceptions and comments are important, not yours.
- For older children, where role playing is too babyish and considered silly, the task is more difficult. It is more difficult because it requires a more analytical approach to ferreting out possible difficulties and more finesse as you go through the process.

Phase I   • List all possible areas of conflict that may exist between the child and each of the family members, including yourself. As in the interference techniques for children for show and tell, enlist the aid of your spouse in a two-parent family or family member or friend in the case of a single-parent family. Make your lists separately and compare and discuss them only when you have each completed your own.

Phase II   • Compare the lists you have generated in Phase I and combine them to come up with a single list. Don't exclude those items on which you cannot come to agreement. List the items from most important to least important.

Phase III   • Once you have generated your lists and compared them and set priorities, you're ready to confront them in terms of ownership. It's entirely possible that the difficulty exists only from the child's perception. This is possible but unlikely, given the degree of experience, life skills, and habits, both positive and negative, that the adult has incorporated into his or her behavior pattern. Once you have determined ownership of the difficulty, parent and child can move into Phase IV, the problem-solving phase.

Phase IV ● Keep in mind that what adults tend to view as problems may not be viewed as such by their children. Therefore, identify whether or not any given situation is viewed as a problem by the child. First, deal with the issues where there is agreement that a problem exists.

Phase V ● Define the problem and set up activities to counter it. Make a contract to follow through on the activities and set up a time within which both you and the child will evaluate the efficacy of those activities.

Chapter Thirteen

The Bitch as Mother

Future Expectations and Present Parenting

The forty-year-old who sat opposite me and talked into my tape recorder seemed to have mastered the ability to view her life in stages while taking care of both the chosen and assigned tasks of parenting with a minimum of hand wringing and an extraordinary amount of pragmatism. That ability and her pragmatic and analytical approach to parenting set Maxine apart from her abdicating sisters.

It is also the major difference between the abdicator and the bitch as mothers.

Maxine: "I don't feel that I'm sacrificing for my kids, and I don't feel that I'm passing my youth. I'm forty. The kids will leave home on a more or less permanent basis in five or six years, so I'll be forty-six. It's no big deal to me. I will always have choices about the men and jobs out there if I want to. If I want a man, I will have one, and if I don't want a man, I won't have one. If I want a different job, I'll have it. I will be an interesting old lady in tennis shoes."

Maxine has three children. Jeff, a son from a previous marriage, is nineteen. Patricia, thirteen, and Joe, fourteen, are from a second marriage. Maxine's second marriage also ended in divorce. After supporting her husband for fifteen years while he attended graduate school—and did not complete his degree—she decided that it was time to take back the role of primary planner for her own life and for her children's lives and to end the marriage.

This is Maxine's response to my question, "Do you sacrifice for your children?"

Maxine: "I haven't taken a nine-to-five job because after the divorce I had to deal with three children who were bereft. But I like being self-employed and making my own hours, so what started out as a modification because of the children became a very good move for me. I don't bring home the men I date because I don't want a lot of traffic in and out. But when I meet someone I plan on spending time with—and after I'm sure he will be in tune with 'love me, love my children'—I let him come home. So I compromise here and there. But I don't see myself as a sacrificing person, because if I sacrifice, I get nasty. I did a lot of sacrificing when I was married, without knowing that's what it was. I don't sacrifice for my children. I compromise."

And it is through modification and compromises that we deliver to our children one of their just deserts: the knowledge that they don't interfere with us but that they interact with us, that they provide us with joys, not jobs.

Without exception, every woman I interviewed and later placed in the category of abdicator as parent viewed her actions as sacrificing.

Those who did not view their behavior as sacrificing exer-

cised a far greater degree of control over their children and
the events that shaped both their lives.

Maxine spoke of the difficulty her younger son, Joe, had in
relating to her.

Maxine: "During the divorce and after it as well, Joe's
father told him I didn't love Joe. There is no question that
Joe felt that he had lost his favorite parent because of the
divorce, and the children knew that I initiated it. Their
father would say in front of the children that I didn't love
Joe, that I should keep Patricia, and that Joe should live
with his father. There was no way that I wanted the children to be separated. They were still learning how to interact with each other, and I considered us a family and
didn't want it broken up. But I had to deal with the fact
that Joe didn't feel comfortable in loving me and that he
didn't want to believe that I loved him. I thought that if he
became close to other women, he'd be able to transfer that
closeness to me. So I encouraged his relationship with his
father's girl friend. As a matter of fact, even when his
father broke up with her, Joe still saw her and he still does.

"I was friendly with another woman who is very aggressive in her affection. I had talked to her about Joe and
we went to visit. Joe wasn't going to come with us but
decided at the last minute to come along. When we went
into the house, I hugged her and whispered to her not to
forget Joe. Well, she didn't, and she hugged him and kept
drawing him into the group. We were sitting down at
dinner and Joe put his hand on my knee and said, 'This is
fun.' He's been making more and more gestures like that
with just me. For example, we went to see "The Day
After" at church and when we were leaving he put his
hand up and straightened my collar. When I looked at
him, I could see that he didn't want me to respond to him.
It would have been like calling someone—and saying,
'See, I told you you love me.'

"We're getting close, but it can't be rushed. For Joe to

know I love him and he loves me means that he'll know his father was wrong. He has to learn that slowly so he'll still love his father. I know that encouraging his relationships with other women—women he sees as mothers—is helping us work out our own relationship."

Rather than Maxine's bemoaning the fact that her son was not able to demonstrate his affection for her or Maxine's denigrating his father to him, she chose to set up situations within which his affection for her could safely be vented without detracting from his positive feeling for his father. In addition, she kept herself attuned to the cues Joe gave out that would allow her to see if her methods were succeeding.

She could have relinquished control over Joe's need. She could have berated his father and boxed herself and Joe into a Ping-Pong match of "I do love you—you don't love me." She could have further stifled his ability to demonstrate love and affection by placing blame on his father. For whatever reason, choosing to place blame results in giving up responsibility. Behaviorally, the choice is a simple one to make when made within the framework of what children deserve, should be permitted to do, and should be allowed to become.

What if it doesn't work—the design, the setup? The answer is persistence. Children should be permitted to question us and not understand our answers the first, second, and third time around; to challenge us and receive careful thought and not reprisal; to build their own value system and not fear its conflict with ours.

Maxine talked about the need for persistence.

Maxine: "I've always given my children a lot of credence. If they said they didn't want something or didn't want me to help, I backed off. That was a mistake, and my older son, Jeff, helped me see this with Joe. One day we were having dinner and someone said something that insulted Joe. He was hurt, left the table, ran out of the room into his bedroom, and slammed the door. I followed after him.

His door was locked, and he said, 'Stay out, get away, get away.' So, fuming, I went back to the dining room. I didn't know what to do. Then Jeff said, 'That would never have stopped you with me, Mom.' So I went back and his door wasn't locked. He wouldn't let me touch him, but I stayed there and I persisted, and after a while, he felt better. Almost all of my breakthroughs with Joe have been because I persisted in the face of tremendous rejection. Persistence works."

Maxine and all of us have choices in these situations. When our children reject our overtures to help them, we can play role reversal, let them have control over the situation, and accept the rejection and not continue the action—or we can persist, take control, and demonstrate not only that we can help but also that we care.

PART THREE

Work

Chapter Fourteen

Making a Living versus Making a Life

Let's begin by setting down three rules all of us know but need to hear repeated.

RULE ONE: **Every field of human endeavor harvests the same number of asses per acre.**

As a woman in the work world you need to recognize them—the congenital asses—if you don't want to be worked over by them. By direct count, you are very likely to collide with the asses in your organization at least once every quarter. These are the times when the budget is due, when performance appraisals are conducted, when "merit" raises are given, when it's time to rephrase your M.B.O.'s, when deadlines are forthcoming, when a new program fails, when a new program succeeds, when there is a change in leadership, when there is a reorganization, when _____. You fill in the blanks.

Some of us deal with these realities as bitches, some deal with them as abdicators. The environment is the same, the reactions—the behavior—is different.

RULE TWO: **Never wound the king—go for the kill or let it be!**

There are many ways to do a halfway job of besting the King in any organization. You can be brighter than he is and tell him so in front of his peers or tell him just between the two of you. You can want his job, and let your ambition be known. You can challenge his decisions, and by doing so, challenge the chain of command.

Abdicators have a tendency to wound the King—and themselves. Bitches co-opt, not kill, the King.

RULE THREE: **Mavericks move molehills and get buried under mountains.**

The majority of corporations and organizations, be they profit-making ones or not-for-profit service organizations, will not tolerate the maverick approach to work activities, regardless of the degree of success that results. Mavericks stray from accepted practices both behaviorally and procedurally. Behaviors that are too far from the norm are viewed with suspicion, and procedures that are short-circuited, no matter how nonproductive or obsolete they may be, raise the red flag of caution.

The bitch has a tendency to practice maverick behaviors, and if she does not understand the company's message, she suffers the consequences of Rule Three.

Abdicators leave maverick behaviors to their more risk-taking sisters.

These three rules apply equally to men and women. There is a difference, however. The man who violates them is often excused; the woman is accused. He is labeled as overzealous and ambitious; she is labeled bitch.

This difference in labeling is accompanied by the gender difference in both expectations and success criteria. First and foremost, at the outset most men are aware that work will be a lifetime endeavor and their advancement is expected not only by themselves but by their organization as well. Women often enter the work world by a more circuitous route. Some enter on what they think will be a temporary basis and only by happenstance find themselves on a career path. Some enter into nonmanagement positions and later, after trial and error, assume supervisory or management positions. It is only in the past decade that large numbers of women have entered the world of work with expectations of advancement, equality of compensation, and increased responsibility and authority—expectations that are not shared by prevailing corporate beliefs.

Given these differences, the woman who wishes to be successful not only must define what success means on a personal level but also must understand what actions she has to take in order to achieve it. She needs to keep these actions in the forefront of her consciousness as she goes about the daily activities and performs the tasks her position requires. She must engage in those actions as though a daily ritual, in order to achieve her success. *She must, quite literally, expend at least 20 percent of her work time engaging in success activities and devote the remaining 80 percent to the tasks required by her job description.*

The experts' definition of success won't do; Mary's definition for success might not be Sally's choice. The definition must be a personal one.

Typing Yourself—Four Classes of Success Criteria

There are many aspects of work life that should be considered within the larger framework of success criteria. We should consider the specific tasks, the areas of responsibility, the degree of authority, and whether we want our technical skills or our managerial skills to be the primary assignment. Superseding all these separate elements of success criteria is the primary goal of where we want to be within the organizational structure.

Through the discussions, interviews, and seminars that I held with over 250 working women, I found four distinctly different categories of this primary goal.

The first category is represented by women who work in management positions and who prefer to maintain their positions at the low- to middle-management level.

The second category is represented by women who are in low- to middle-management positions and who desire upward mobility within their organizations.

The third category includes women who, in addition to holding midmanagement positions and seeking upward mobility, had achieved a level of recognized expertise in their career area.

The fourth and last category comprises women who work in mid- or upper management, desire upward mobility, are recognized experts, and who express the need for increased discretionary authority within their work activities.

Regardless of the category they choose, women face a set of obstacles to their goals very different from that faced by men.

- Women who prefer to remain at their present level are faced with the double-bind message that says, *Be aggressive. Be ambitious—even though you want to stay where you are.* These women need to learn how to display enthusiasm, energy, and aggressive behavior without acting on it, so that they appear to carry out the company message and thus do away with the obstacle that is in the way of their personal success.

- For the women in the second category, those who wish upward mobility, the double-bind message is, *Upward mobility for you means a terminal position below that of your male counterpart and only within certain areas of the organization.* These women need to learn behaviors that will cause them to be viewed as workers, not as women, in order to eliminate the obstacle that is in the way of their personal success.

● For the third category, the recognized experts, the double-bind message is, *You are now typecast. Stay there.* This is a message very different from that offered to her male counterpart, who is given opportunities to learn and to develop his potential in areas outside his demonstrated expertise. These women need to learn methods and behaviors that will give them discretionary authority over the tasks they are given.

● For the fourth category, the women who desire personal freedom within their work activities, the double-bind message is, *Think creatively, but follow the book.* In this instance, a similar message is offered to their male counterparts, with one difference. For the male counterpart, the need for maximizing his freedom is accepted; hers is not. These women need to practice behaviors that will allow them to appear to accommodate to the company message of freedom so that they can do what they must in order to meet their success goal.

Make no mistake about it—women are still treated differently from men in the world of work. They are paid less in spite of executive orders and affirmative action. They are locked out of job classifications in spite of the job descriptions' lack of bona fide occupational qualifications. They are still labeled with different and down-grading cultural value assessments, in spite of the women's movement, networking, and publicity engendered by past ERA efforts.

Different success criteria require different behaviors if success is to be achieved. Different messages require different behaviors if we are to offset the limits and restraints that these messages impose.

Different organizational beliefs, attitudes, expectations, and actions about and toward women require different behaviors if those beliefs, attitudes, expectations, and actions are to be changed.

The Company Climate

Choosing the appropriate behaviors to deal with these differences requires a working understanding of the corporate climate. The corporate climate is composed of the general rules of organizational life, the specific messages of your organization, and the differences practiced by your organization with respect to men and women. When these areas are understood, you can modify your behavior and use the rules and differences to your advantage.

Rather than use prior understandings of corporate climates or gather the information only from the women I was interviewing, I decided to report on the current state of these rules and practices by getting them from individuals who had the power to enforce the rules and were in a position to witness the practices. Since this was the sole criterion I used in choosing interviewees for this section, it should not be surprising that the majority of them were men.

Serendipitously, at about the time that I was searching for the right—read honest—people to interview, I received a call from a professional recruiter who asked for my help in locating an individual to fill a high-level position in a Fortune 500 company. The position offered compensation in the $60,000 range, and the individual chosen would be groomed to head the organizational development department in a vice-presidential capacity.

This is what he said:

Peter: "Toni, I need to fill this position with a man. The company said they want someone who can relate to their kind of people. They are after someone who wants money, drinks, and chases women."

He went on to say that, although he knew that my professional qualifications were just what the company was looking for, they did not want a woman. I wasn't surprised by the conversation because this wasn't the first time he had called me with that request. We made a trade. I gave him some names, and he gave me the following statement in a taped interview, as well as some leads for interviews with individuals he believed would not just give me the "human relations" line but would be honest in their discussions of the corporate restraints that are being placed on women because of their sex.

Peter: "Women cannot afford to fail at the same things that men are permitted to fail at in any organization. Women can't be prissy or too sweet, but they have to stay on the pedestal where the society has placed them, even though there are some industries that won't hire them because they still adhere to the pedestal concept of womanhood. They have to be better than the men at their jobs, and one way of showing this is to know the job of the people under you.

"Many women today are brought in above entry level and have not worked themselves up through the ranks. This makes companies believe that they are not as capable of either the job they've been given or the job above them, so they get terminally positioned and don't have the chance men have for upward mobility.

"Women have to learn to stand their ground and speak their piece. They have to be objective and realistic and protect their vulnerability with facts. It should be no surprise that women are making it to the top in market research, for example, because the company has to look at the facts, not at a subjective opinion. Any job that carries with it more subjective analysis as opposed to the presentation of facts that everyone can see and taste is going to be a difficult one for a woman to succeed in.

"Upper-echelon positions require subjective analysis; they require decision making and policy formation. These are subjective aspects, not objective. When subjective analyses are called for, the company is more prone to view the woman as a woman and not as a worker."

Peter has a three-point program of advice for women who want to succeed in corporate structures.

1. *Be better at what you do than your male counterpart.* If you think this sounds like an injustice or a lack of equality because you have to be "more equal," then congratulate yourself. You're thinking on the right track. If you want to follow point one of Peter's three-point plan, you have a lot of homework ahead of you.

Read the trade journals. Call someone who has your position at one of your company's major competitors and pick his or her brains. All of this you do on your time for homework, not on company time. These are the actions that your success requires. Going to women's meetings and discussing the relevant inequalities and injustices that are practiced by your respective companies may be informative, but it will help only to escalate your frustration and, more important, will take time away from the actions that you should be taking to increase your expertise and your success.

There will be time enough to do away with the injustices and inequalities when you are the CEO.

2. *In all things, be objective.* Remove the "I" message from your language. Neither your boss nor your co-workers share the relationship that you have with your husband or lover—and if they do, they shouldn't. Husbands and lovers get the "I" message. Bosses and co-workers get the following:

- "The situation calls for . . ."
- "These items need to be reevaluated"
- "An analysis of the three contrasting approaches shows that . . ."

In other words, objectify your language pattern, remove the personal pronouns.

In your memos and written reports, use the old college essay outline form:

- There are three components that require separate and distinct approaches.

- Each of these components has three to five items that have been investigated.
- Component I. Widget rejection analysis
- Item 1. Of the *twenty-three* (23) widgets that were rejected, *four* (4) of them were found to have sharp edges, *seventeen* (17) were two shades darker than the acceptable tone, and the remaining *two* (2) were off scale by two degrees.
- Item 2. All *twenty-three* (23) widgets were produced during the night shift.

You get the point—objectify, structure, and quantify whenever possible. Attach a summary chart. A summary always appears on the first page. It gives the bottom-line information that has been requested. You have also covered all bases by presenting your summary in the beginning, and there is less chance that you'll be pulled off the track by someone's focus on his pet problem. Once they get started on that pet problem, the value of your analysis, as well as your abilities, gets lost. Remember, everyone has another meeting to go to. Giving the summary up front helps to bring your presentation to a close, which again shows that you've met the objective by being objective.

3. *Stand your ground and speak your piece.* Imagine the following scenario. You are sitting in a meeting room with five other people. One of them is a co-worker, another is your boss, two of them are your boss's peers, and the one remaining, situated at the head of the conference table, is his boss. You have worked on the project that is being discussed, and you have valid contributions to make to the discussion.

- Look at your watch; tell yourself that you will participate in the meeting within the first fifteen minutes, and do it.
- Don't let yourself be intimidated by the conference room or its occupants.
- The first time it's like going to the dentist; the second time around, you won't need as much Novocain, and by the third time, you'll be comfortable.

- You're getting paid to speak your piece, and doing what you're paid to do is the first step toward success.

I have personally counseled over 1,000 managers, from CEO level down to entry level. In keeping with work realities, 75 percent of these managers were men, and they were all afraid at some point in their careers to speak their piece and stand their ground. Those who did so, in spite of their fears, were successful; those who didn't, were not.

I have seen men grow gray with fear in corporate boardrooms. The stress of meeting deadlines or of implementing new procedures was met with anxiety. The fear of speaking up, presenting a nonpopular view, and being ridiculed, either overtly or covertly, was decimating. They often sat like grade-school children, shrinking from the possibility of being called on by the teacher and not having the right answer.

Their fear was unrecognized; they were thought instead to be uncommunicative—*which was true*. The increase in their heart rate that fear produced was unrecognized; they were thought to be nonparticipative—*which was true*. The insecurity they felt about their jobs was unrecognized; they were thought to be nonteam players—*which was true*.

That fear was the motivating factor behind this abdicating behavior went unrecognized. What was recognized was that they weren't doing the job.

Peter's three-point program for success is a combination of both work and image building. Both are important. The work component and the development of increased expertise, while time consuming, generally present few problems. We have been in training for the job content since we began our careers. You can read trade journals, study reports, and keep up with new concepts and ideas in your field in the privacy of your bedroom while you paint your toenails.

The image building—using the right behavioral strategy— is far more difficult. One-shot seminars on how to dress, speak, and play the corporate game successfully are but short-term in their effect if not practiced daily. You need to do it in the boardroom, do it in the lunch room, do it at the water cooler, and do it in the elevator.

Bitches do it, abdicators don't. Without the appropriate behavioral strategy, you can amass all of the technical skills in your field and your career will still not be successful.

The following story from George, director of personnel and training of a Fortune 500 firm, describes a classic case of poor image building.

> <u>George:</u> "She was fired from a top-level job. The problem was that every time she got up to talk to a group of managers, she pissed them off. She came across as pompous, as a know-it-all, the expert who had all the answers. It wasn't that she was stupid, she wasn't, but she prided herself so much on her professional knowledge that she diminished the need to have folks respect her expertise and her value to them as someone who considers other people. She just didn't come across as though she *cared* about doing a job for them."

Coming across as pompous, pissing people off, and not being valued as a helper of others are all behaviors that translate into not being political. George continued his discussion with his definition of political realities.

> <u>George:</u> "Being political is creating a network of relationships that can help you get the job done. It's an unofficial directory that you keep with you at all times. It tells you who has pockets of information and special abilities that will help you do your job more effectively. It's having people like you, having them see you as a person of influence. It's doing them favors and letting them know that they can call on you for favors. That's politics, getting people to help you get the job done."

Being political is also showing loyalty. George talked about how the definition of loyalty in his corporation had changed with a change in leadership and about the part of loyalty that will never change in any organization.

> *George:* "We have a new CEO, and I'm sensing a change in the definition of loyalty to the company. Before he came on board, loyalty meant being a consistent trooper and being there. With our new CEO, loyalty means . . . Hey, stick to your guns and look out for the best interests of the company. If you see business opportunities in your area, then it's your responsibility to speak up.
>
> "Of course, numero uno is always the boss; you can't end-run the boss, that's disastrous. You have to examine the opportunities that you see and get your boss to go along with you. But remember that the boss comes first. If you don't, then you're not seen as being loyal. You're seen as a troublemaker."

George did more here than simply define loyalty and restate the Never Wound the King rule. Knowing that the climate changes with changes in leadership means having political savvy. Translating your political savvy into action requires that you find out all you can about the new leader. Talk to people from his last company, get his bio (it's in the company library). Seek out people in your company who are known as politically astute and shrewd. Go to lunch with them and get the lay of the land.

Here again, political realities are a combination of both work and behavior—the work that it takes to research the leaders and gather information from the politically astute, and the behavior that it takes to form a network of relationships with people who can help you get the job done.

Success is the result of combining the two within the corporate climate. The paradox often inherent in the directive to do the best job for the company and to remain loyal to the boss first, the department second, and the company third can be solved, according to George, by "salesmanship."

I asked George what to do about the dilemma of being given a responsibility without having the authority to carry it out.

George: "When you are given a responsibility and you don't have the power or the authority to carry it out, it puts the premium on salesmanship. In selling, you have to have your homework done—the rational and logical aspects of whatever the project is about—but you also have to believe in what you are doing. You have to show that enthusiasm or crusadership.

"In fact, I had a manager who told me, 'I don't need an advocate, I need a crusader.' He was telling me about one of his people. He said that the fellow believes in the company's product but doesn't have the energy level, or the persistence; he doesn't explore the opportunities to sell it and to tell the story and to get it across. A good salesman will stick to his guns to get the story across within the political realities."

Once again, a combination of work, the "rational and logical" aspects of the project—remember that rationality and logic can be demonstrated behaviorally by keeping your language free of personal pronouns and using those objective words—and behavior, the behavior of salesmanship.

If you look closely at that definition of salesmanship—energy, enthusiasm, persistence, tell the story, get it across—you can begin to trace a one-to-one relationship between the definition and the behaviors.

Energy:
- Walk and talk faster.
- Raise and lower the tone of your voice for emphasis.
- Wear a splash of bright colors or use bright colors as accents.
- Use purposeful body movements—light a cigarette, get an ashtray, pour yourself a cup of coffee, open the window, close the window, make appropriate gestures.

The key is that movement translates into energy, regardless of how lethargic or nonenergetic you really feel.

Enthusiasm:
- Flash your eyes.
- Change your facial expression.
- Verbalize enthusiasm. ("I'm enthused about this," "I can't wait to get into this," "This really turns me on.")

Persistence:
- Follow it up with a memo.
- Talk about it at lunch.
- Make another phone call to follow up on your memo.
- Remember that persistence shows up better in person-to-person contact.

You don't have to be a crusader in order to act like one, any more than Jack Nicholson had to be psychotic when he won an Oscar for *One Flew Over the Cuckoo's Nest.* He "acted" crazy, and you can act as though you are 100 percent behind a project, even though on a scale of one to ten you have only a 2.5 percent enthusiasm quotient for it. In the old days, we would call these pretenses women's wiles. Today we might call them communication skills. Label them what you will, we need to display those responses that will allow us to both look and act the part. If this is criminal, then so be it. If we need to learn how to stick to our guns, then we'd best move from poacher to sheriff and work our wiles to enhance our power and add to our paycheck.

There is a cornucopia of rewards handed out when selling skills are used, and in all corporations there is an informal system of rewards and punishments that must be recognized if the punishments are to be avoided and the rewards are to be actively sought. George explained the reward-and-punishment system practiced in his company.

George: "Aside from the obvious set of rewards—a larger budget, more people in your department, merit increases, and bonuses—there are others, such as the amount of time that the boss spends with you and how often he seeks your counsel and your advice on the department issues. It is a negotiable reward because you are seen as a person of influence if the boss is known to seek you out and rely on your input. It also goes back to the discussion of loyalty: when you are being perceived as someone who helps out the boss, it helps you gather your network of political helpers.

"In addition to the time issue, another reward is being included on a project at the outset or at an early stage. We had a situation just recently where the reverse was true. One of my counterparts was punished by not being told what was going on, and it directly concerned his area. He wasn't even asked for input. When that got out, he became a pariah. When that happens, when you get put on a blacklist, you lose your credibility, you lose your influence, and you lose whatever network you've been able to develop. That changes your effectiveness; it stops you from doing your job."

At the close of the interview with George, I asked him what advice he would give his daughter if she were to join his company as a new manager.

George: "First, find out what your boss's objectives are. What are his priorities. Then I would begin with networking, gathering the people that you will need to help you get your job done. Be sensitive to those of your peers who are rewarded and those who are punished. Follow a monkey-see, monkey-do attitude. Emulate the ones who are being rewarded as well as bring your own personal creativity to your job. Avoid the ones who are being punished. There's something to the 'birds of a feather flock together' maxim.

"There is always someone who needs you to get your job done so that he can get his job done. Instead of thinking about your work as a product, think of it as a service—

a service that you perform for those around you to enable their jobs to get done. This helps you create your network, and it helps you to be viewed as a team player.

"There are times when you genuinely have to give up your principles in order to get the job done. If you are going to be successful, you have to face that reality. If there is one difference between men and women that I see, it is that women are more sensitive than men are; they take things personally. When I think of giving advice to my daughter, I think about her strengths and her weaknesses. She is hardworking and committed to her work, but she is overly sensitive to the opinions of others. If I were to counsel her how to deal with that issue, I would say, 'Try to think like a man.' No, I really wouldn't say that in a million years, but its the first thing that comes to my mind."

George had some good advice for the woman who chooses to be successful within the corporate structure. However, rather than "think like a man" where sensitivities are the issue, the woman who would be successful should exercise her choices so that she can take control rather than relinquish control as does the abdicator.

Taking control will often put her on trial: "She acts like a man," "She's too aggressive," "She won't take 'shit' from anyone," "She's a bitch." Relinquishing control will put her career plans in the hands of an inequitable system at best.

There are clearly different choices and very different results between abdication and control. When the woman at work chooses to abdicate, she violates the rules of corporate life, does not adhere to the company message, and, ostrich-like, pretends that corporate practices are applied to men and women on an equal basis.

Come meet the abdicator as she plays Pollyanna with her work priorities and clothes herself for the boardroom in behavioral frills best saved for the bedroom.

Chapter Fifteen

Abdicators at Work–Bitches Need Not Apply

Denise: "I felt like a horse they were trying to break. I was having my performance appraisal, which was being conducted by my immediate supervisor and his boss. This wasn't the usual procedure, having the appraisal conducted by two levels of management above me, but it was being done this way because my previous boss had been transferred to another department. He was transferred because of the disagreements between us.

"Throughout the whole appraisal I felt like a horse that they were trying to break. I should have told them how I felt, and I should have told them what the disagreements were between me and my first boss. I didn't want to talk about him because he wasn't there to defend himself, and I didn't want to tell them how I felt because I was afraid I'd lose my job. Eventually I did lose it; my new boss said that if anyone asked me why, just tell them that I wanted his job and I couldn't have it. I would have felt a lot better about losing the job if I had at least stood up for myself. As it happened, when I was fired, I had an anxiety attack."

If one word were needed to characterize Denise's career, it would be *diverse*. Her experience has spanned the gamut from marketing training programs for educational institutions to conducting affirmative action and job equity seminars for major corporations. After completing her formal education to the master's degree level, she taught in a university system and held the position of assistant professor in political science and designed management programs in information retrieval, personal management, and career mobility.

In Denise's case, all systems were "technically" correct; her credentials and abilities were never in question. She short-circuited herself with her behavior. The bottom-line result was that her behavior caused her to forfeit a $35,000-a-year position plus the possibility of upward mobility within the company.

Denise: "After the performance appraisal, I seriously thought of taking out a loan on my house, putting the cash in the bank, and going for broke at work. I felt that if I had some extra cash behind me then I'd be willing to say what I meant and stand up for what I thought was right for the department. I had already proved that I was capable of doing it, and it was frustrating as hell having to put up with doing a half-assed con job and showing up on Saturdays for what some people called face time.

"One of my co-workers told me to come in on Saturday, put my briefcase on my desk, scatter some papers around, and then leave and do what I had to do and come back and get my briefcase so that it would look like I was in on Saturday.

"I hated having to go to meetings that were called at 5:30, at the last minute, with no agenda or notice. My boss was just responding to a shoot-from-the-hip suggestion from his boss. We just wasted our time. It was horrible. I hated the situation and loved the tasks, but they wouldn't let me do them."

The pattern of Denise's abdicating behavior included *lack of confrontation, of both feelings and facts; a need to keep the "nice guy" self-image; and fear of risk taking. In addition, she violated the Never Wound the King rule and refused to adhere to the company message.* Let's take a closer look at these behaviors.

She did not confront her supervisor or his boss during the performance appraisal with respect to her feeling "like a horse they were trying to break." Obviously she was being asked to comply with a company norm. She neglected to invite the feedback she needed in order to discover exactly what they wanted her to comply with. She allowed her emotions to override her need to know.

If confrontation is difficult in love relationships and in parenting, it is far more difficult in a business situation where there is a definite boundary of power over and through which we need to tread carefully.

The strategy here is to invite feedback and get the other person's point of view without incurring his or her wrath.

Here are questions that will invite feedback:

- "What the hell do you mean by that?"
- "You are making me feel like shit."
- "I'm confused; I'm not sure that I understand what you mean. Can you explain it to me?"

It is not difficult to figure out which is the best approach, especially when you're not in the power position.

In addition to neglecting to confront the situation, Denise also withheld factual information that could have been used to her advantage because her ex-boss "wasn't there to defend himself." She kept the "nice guy" image, forgetting that there are definite distinctions between the corporate self and the personal self.

Corporate ethics follow the golden rule that says, "He who has the gold (power) rules." Corporate ethics require that you be bitchy enough to do unto others before they do unto you. Sounds terrible? Sounds nasty? Perhaps, but it is also what the woman who chooses success must understand, and her actions must follow her understanding.

I want the message to be quite clear here: *I am advocating situational behavior not behavioral rules in the absolute.* In a love relationship, marital or otherwise, the golden rule you were taught as a child holds, provided you are receiving love, caring, and support in kind. In love relationships, the issue is equality. In parenting, you are serving as a role model, and the issue is the strength that you have by virtue of the fact that you are the adult.

In work relationships, the issue is *authority,* and you don't have the benefit of either alleged or actual equality of power. In work situations, there is limited room at the top, and there is limited room where you are at the moment.

Nice guys finish last, and nice women come in second to the nice guys. This is especially true when you remember the double-bind messages through which the corporation differentiates between men and women.

The corporate woman who is successful does not behave with her co-workers or superiors as she would with her husband or lover.

The corporate woman who is successful does not behave with her co-workers or superiors as she would with her children.

The corporate woman who is successful modifies her behavior according to the situation that she finds in the world of work and makes no apologies for the fact that she is after *power* in addition to equality, and *authority* in addition to strength.

She accepts the label *bitch* with pleasure and pride and denies that her behavior is either terrible or nasty. Unlike Denise, she is also able to take risks. Fear or risk taking is the underlying motivation of abdicating behavior. In her case, Denise had the wherewithal to take the risk, understood what to do in order to initiate it, didn't take it, and lost not only her job but also a good chunk of her self-confidence in the process.

The behavioral strategies to offset the difficulties of risk taking are clear:

- Set yourself up financially as soon as you are able to meet your financial needs—needs, not wants—for at least six months of unemployment.
- If you have the financial ability, use it when a calculated risk is called for. Take stock in yourself, and consider your risk as you would an investment in the market.
- If a "what if" question results in a "I might lose my job" answer, remember that it's better to lose a job for the right reasons and be left with your self-confidence intact than to lose it for somebody else's right reasons.

Taking calculated risks is a must for success, especially for women who are still viewed with pedestal value systems and are tried for their bitchiness. Where risk taking is involved, I cannot help but agree with the French revolutionist and philosopher Saint-Just, who said, "She who builds the revolution only halfway builds her own tomb." (I have taken some license here with the gender in Saint-Just's quote.)

When Denise violated the Never Wound the King rule, she compounded the violation by playing nice guy and not "going for broke." With a pattern like that, she couldn't have scripted her demise better. Here's how she did it:

Denise: "I challenged him [her ex-boss]. I'm not sure if I did it because I was being idealistic and believed that it was all right to disagree with him and take over his responsibilities or if I did it because I was so infuriated. The whole situation was a disaster.

"There were several meetings where we would discuss a proposal or a task at length and the discussion seemed to go on forever. I'm very good at organizing and structuring work and issues. I simply took over the meetings and organized and delegated work and got it done. I did it when we were working on issues that were internal to the department and when his peers were at meetings as well. Now I wish I had been sure of my motives. I honestly tried to protect my first boss, and after he was transferred, I went out of my way to support his replacement publicly, though I told him when I thought he was wrong when we were alone. I did consciously take control of meetings. I was showing off and I got shoved out."

Having shown "disloyalty," by corporate definition, to her first boss, her second boss was not about to give any power to her. His witnessing of her takeovers during meetings at which he presided only increased her "disloyalty quotient" for him. It's no wonder that Denise's second boss told her, "If anyone asks you why you were fired, tell them that you wanted my job and couldn't have it." Denise in retrospect said that she wished she had been more sure of her motives.

Had she kept in focus her success criterion—upward mobility within the company—she might not have violated so many of the rules of a club she professed she wanted not only to join but in which she wanted to become a leader. To fear taking risks, to emotionally hold onto a nice-guy image, and to ego-indulge when objectivity is the better route to power do not a leader make. By her own admission, Denise hated the situation but loved the task. By her behavior, she escalated the frustrations inherent in the situation and was prevented from performing the task. As the joke goes—"The job had no future. I was fired."

An aside is necessary here with regard to the ego-indulging monster that takes hold of us and the strategies that can protect us against its bite.

- Don't expect ego strokes to come along except on pay and power day—there is a one-to-one relationship that operates between pay and power. If you get ego strokes along the way, consider them icing.
- Take care where you shop for ego strokes. Several of the women I interviewed, myself included, quite can-

didly admitted that the reason their closets are filled
with silk blouses and suede suits or their homes cluttered with goodies—I have been told that I have de-
clared war on space—was not so much they they needed
the items but that they were compensating themselves
for the rewards that were not forthcoming at work.

- Frustration level at work is directly proportional to
  plastic indebtedness, and that disease can prevent you
  from accumulating the financial wherewithal to take
  that calculated risk when you deem it necessary.
- Buy stocks, buy property, with someone else's money
  if possible; let your boss's wife be the high roller at Saks.

Denise helped to insure that her boss's wife could continue
to be the high roller at Saks by violating not only general
corporate rules but the specific climate of her copmpany as
well.

The company climate was obvious: show up on Saturdays—it makes the boss look good; be enthusiastic at late-
night meetings—it makes you part of the "hardworking
team"; if they ask for a plan, give them ten—even when you
know that nine of them are not feasible; you're on straight
salary, but you're being told to do piecework—snow them
with paper. This was the company climate, and those were
the company messages. By not buying them, Denise was
typed as an inefficient player in the political arena.

The point here is that *you can't behave as though you have the
discretionary authority to ignore the company messages until you
have the power to do so.*

Being successful means making choices, and if you choose
not to follow the company line, then you have not chosen
success—at least not in that company. Going along allows
you to get along. Denise chose not to go along when she
chose to disregard the company messages, and as a result, the
company did not regard her as a dues-paying member.

These messages violated Denise's need for personal freedom and produced not only conflict but obstacles between
her personal freedom needs, upward mobility goals, and

achievement needs of getting the job done "as fast as best I could," instead of as fast and as best as the company required. That productivity for this company was hindered by the company message I do not deny. That Denise's demise in the company was a result of her refusal to dress herself for the company climate no one can deny.

If the corporate woman approaches her job with intensity and believes that any more than 50 percent of the tasks that she performs are worth while, then she will both alienate and intimidate both her co-workers and her superiors—especially if she is good at what she does. When you alienate the power brokers and play rate breaker with your team members, you cannot be successful in the present climate of the American industrial montage.

One of the corporate dilemmas that causes this reality is that implicit in all job descriptions are *assigned* tasks in addition to the *chosen* tasks. It is in these assigned tasks that the company message and company climate is found. Most frequently, assigned tasks have little to do with the overall productivity of the company except to hinder it, and it is through the purging of assigned tasks that new leadership and new fads usually produce an immediate increase in both overall efficiency and productivity. Unfortunately, these benefits are often short-lived as new messages and new climates develop.

These conflicts not only cause the able and productive individual to lose her job—when she refuses to go along to get along—they also cause the company to lose a truly loyal worker. When the company is such that it adheres to face time, busy work, and piecework climate and applauds a "snow them with paper" mentality, it contributes to the American industrial dilemma that denies the benefits able and productive people have to offer.

Chapter Sixteen

"I Can't Be That Way"

I can't dress for the company climate, I can't carry the company message, and "I can't be that way." Perhaps this is the section that will allow George to give more succinct advice to his daughter than to "think like a man." We can write as many books as the market will bear, we can give as many seminars as can be conducted, we can be as liberated and as aware as both our souls and our experience will allow, but if we hold to the "I can't be that way" belief, our books, seminars, liberation, and awareness will amount to naught. Gloria's story shows the damages of the "I can't be that way" attitude of the abdicator.

Gloria is twenty-three. She is exceptionally attractive and is a merchandise secretary in a large retail organization. She is as bright as she is attractive. She holds a midmanagement position and is seeking upward mobility within her organization. The company climate is such that movement up the management ladder is rarely attained from the position that she at present holds. Fortunately for Gloria, the manager within her division has recognized her potential and does not follow the informal rules of the organization that deny advancement to merchandise secretaries, considering them to be terminally placed. Unfortunately, the manager is four levels above Gloria and is not always on the scene to run interference. Though Gloria was in a good position to ask for his support, her "I can't be that way" behavior prevented her from requesting it. Gloria's present goal is to be promoted to the position of assistant buyer. As merchandise secretary, she is required to process the paperwork, highlight potential problem areas, and follow through on the tasks of the assistant buyer, who is her immediate supervisor.

> *Gloria:* "He makes all kinds of sexual references. He's married and new in town. His wife hasn't moved into town yet, and every time he makes a comment, I feel so embarrassed. He also keeps telling me that's not the way he was used to processing his work at _____. I've tried to tell him how we do it here, and every time we get into a conversation he makes a pass or tells me how his previous company did it. I know how one of the other merchandise secretaries handles him. She tells him where to get off. I heard them go at it once. She really told him off. I just couldn't be that way. She went into this long women's lib stuff. I'm not like that. I'm not a feminist. I just want to do my job, and I know that I can do the job of an assistant buyer. We didn't have one in the department for nine months, and I did everything that an assistant buyer does."

I asked Gloria if she was made acting assistant buyer during that time or if she had received any additional salary or other compensation while she was doing the work of an assistant buyer. "No, but I did all the work, even though it meant I was working overtime a lot."

In Gloria's position, company policy states that overtime must be compensated for. Gloria was aware of this and yet took no action. "I thought they would see just what I could do and that it would help me get a promotion. If I asked for overtime money, they might have thought I was being pushy. I just can't be that way."

Gloria practiced two of the behaviors often displayed by the abdicator at work. First, she did not confront the violation of her rights as an individual with regard to the sexual harassment that she was subjected to nor did she confront the violations of company policy that caused her to lose compensation that was her due. Rather than be viewed as "being pushy," she allowed both these affronts—personal and business—to continue.

What concerns us here is not what caused Gloria to feel that she "can't be that way," but how she can behave in such a way as to confront the wrongs done her and insure her rights in spite of her beliefs and feelings. In work situations, just as in love relationships and in parenting, *behavioral change precedes attitudinal change.* Gloria experienced feelings common to young women at the beginning of their careers. Indeed, her fears are not very different from those experienced by hundreds of both men and women I have counseled. She felt embarrassed by the sexual comments, she was shy, and she was fearful of attending to her rights. Feelings of embarrassment and shyness can be painful, and more important, in the work world they can prevent us from using our capabilities and reaching our potential.

The first step in acting out in spite of these feelings is to recognize that you don't hold a monopoly on them. The second step is to confront them both personally and with the individual or group that causes you to respond with shyness, embarrassment, or fear.

In the face of feelings of shyness and embarrassment, it is far easier to confront violations when you are aware that the violation is not a personal affront but instead one that is practiced across the board. Understanding the rights, privileges, and perks of your position, as they apply to everyone in the organization who holds the same or similar positions, gives you group membership rights. Group membership rights remove the violation from the subjective and personal realm and allow you to confront them on an objective basis. There is every reason to assume that Gloria's immediate supervisor would practice sexual harassment with any woman who struck his fancy. He did not single her out. Similarly, an organization that permits an individual to assume the duties of a position requiring more accountability and withholds commensurate compensation will violate its pay policy whenever the situation calls for it. Gloria was not singled out for this violation. It is a standard practice of the company for which she worked. This takes the violation away from the "I can't be that way," "I can't say that," "I can't fight it" realm and places it into "the policy is being violated" context.

Individuals have less difficulty voicing an objection to the violation of a company policy than confronting a personal injustice. The other benefit is that once you have accustomed yourself to dealing with objective concerns it is easier to counter and confront personal difficulties. There are two strategies that Gloria could have used in spite of her feelings and in the face of the situation.

First, Gloria could have *used confrontative language that kept the violation of her rights in the objective realm.*

- "The policy was not being followed with respect to overtime when I assumed the role of assistant buyer" instead of "I was not getting overtime when I deserved it."
- "His language was unacceptable in a business environment" instead of "He made sexual remarks to me and made me embarrassed."

Second, she could have *used the power she had with the division head.* Gloria's situation was such that she could easily have gotten the ear of the division head. He was aware of her potential, and he had served as a mentor to others in her situation. He was outspoken against the type of harassment that Gloria's supervisor was practicing—he had a daughter in the company. Gloria had the power to enlist his help and didn't. Her reasons were "I didn't want to appear pushy" and "I'm not a feminist." Just as her abdicator sisters do in marital and love relationships, she allowed other people to define what her behavior should be by accepting the negative labels applied to aggressive behavior when it is displayed by women.

Chapter Seventeen

Settling for Nonnegotiable Rewards

Georgia also displayed abdicating behavior, some of which mirrored Gloria's, but with the addition that she settled for nonnegotiable rewards, adopted a nice-guy attitude, and set for herself a mission that was bound to be unsuccessful in the corporate world.

I interviewed Georgia at her office. It was neat and efficient-looking with a clean desk top. The required picture of son and hubby was off to one side, a well-trained rubber plant stood in one corner, and a personal file cabinet with a silent digital clock was in another. Without the window and carpeting that weren't offered as perks at her level, Georgia's office bore all the marks of studied sterility found in the cubbies of the cadres of midmanagement personnel.

Georgia is thirty-six years old, is married, and has one child, a three-year-old son. Her husband is on dropoff duty, and she runs the pickup service for her son's nursery school. Being on pickup duty often interferes with the development of political networks, the gathering of information, and the general camaraderie that take place after work. This is only one of the obstacles faced at work by the woman with a family. Another and more serious obstacle, because it is not under her control to solve, is the unspoken message at Georgia's company that families exist for the support of the executive manager, whereas women work to add to the support of their families. Given this assumed dichotomy, it's no wonder that in Georgia's company, and in many others like it, there are eyebrows raised in question when hubby and son are displayed in the corporate woman's office, and pursed lips and attaboy smiles when the same photo is seen in the office of her male counterpart.

Georgia began her professional life as a pediatric nurse.

Georgia: "When I saw that I was not receiving the respect I felt I deserved, that I was not being listened to, and that I didn't have the freedom to perform my job as I thought it should be done, I went ahead and got my master's in nursing. I thought I had to increase my abilities. Actually, after I got my master's I still didn't get the respect and rewards I felt the position deserved."

The first clue to Georgia's abdicating pattern was that in her first job she started the process of looking only to herself as the cause for "not receiving the respect I thought the position deserved." There is no doubt that an additional degree and formal education are useful—Georgia's mistake was to believe that the problems inherent in the system that treats physicians as all-knowing and nurses as slaves would change if she increased her skill level. She had the "If I change, the system will give me what I want" philosophy, very similar to Gloria's "If I show them I can do the job, they will automatically reward me." I am struck by how similar this belief is to that of the battered wife who tells herself, "If I don't do anything that will upset him, he won't hit me." Here again, it's the belief that the situation is completely personalized, that it operates somehow mysteriously differently if you can learn the right button to press. Not so when you're the only one who is making the effort.

When Georgia realized that the system was preventing her from achieving the rewards she sought, she decided to make a career change, took a degree in counseling, and prepared herself for a career in organizational development. At present, she holds a managerial position in a prestigious Fortune 500 firm.

Georgia told me about her job and how she handles it.

Georgia: "The divisions that are in my jurisdiction have a lot of little pieces. There are several departments, and they all have different problems. I find myself going around and picking up pieces, a small project here, a little gig there. I almost never say no to any of the requests that come into my division. As a result, I give up my image as an expert and as a calm worker. Since I'm doing a lot of little things and there is low visibility to them, I'm always frazzled and I'm not seen as creative or innovative. I simply need to say no to the little ones and go after the projects that will give me visibility."

In addition to settling for nonnegotiable rewards by picking up little pieces and never saying no, Georgia had problems being aggressive and getting the information she needed in order to do her job.

Georgia: "I'm not assertive enough. I have to be able to go into someone's office and barge in while they're working. My peer, the boy wonder, does just that. I do things like 'I need to see you, pretty please.' I feel as though it's not courteous to just barge in, so I say 'If you're busy, I don't want to bother you,' and then wait for them to follow up and call me back, which they rarely do. I should say, 'I have something here that I need some information on or I need feedback on.' It's partly because I want to be courteous and partly because I don't feel valued or valuable enough."

Georgia feels that her behavior of never saying no and of going around and picking up the little pieces is the result of the nice-guy image women are trained to adopt. When she contrasted her mission on the job and the rewards she wanted with those of her male counterpart, it was obvious that it was more the mission that she chose than her socialization that kept her from achieving the success that she said she wanted.

> *Georgia:* "My co-worker's mission is to be a change agent, but most of this is personal. He's in it for himself, and he's in it to go places. He wants a promotion every two years, and he wants to make more money. My mission is different. I want to do something that's relevant. I want to help other managers manage better. We spend a lot of time in the work place, and it's important to train and develop managers to handle people properly. I basically think that organizations and management need a lot of help, and if I have a mission, that's what I'm about."

Indeed, Georgia was living up to and receiving nonnegotiable rewards that were implicit in her mission. But when the promotions and the ratings didn't come, she blamed it on the inequalities in the organization rather than on the difference between her purpose or mission and that of her co-worker who was getting all the promotions that she felt she was entitled to.

Georgia was giving the organization what she believed to be relevant, and very possibly it was. But she was also hindering her own advancement with the nice-guy image, picking up little pieces, and choosing low-visibility projects, which though necessary detracted from her image.

The primary conflict in Georgia's story is the difference

between what the company believes a successful manager should look like and what Georgia believes the company needs with respect to her work area. She did not behave as a success. She behaved as a helper, not as a manager. She did not seek success; she sought gratification that her work was worth while and then became confused and angry when she was not successful. The bottom line for Georgia is that she was not giving the company what they wanted. She was giving them what she wanted them to take from her.

Georgia's is but one of many stories that point out the disturbing fact that work gratification and success—success measured in moving up the corporate ladder—do not go hand in hand. Her story is representative of a significant difference in the behaviors and goals between the many men and women that I counseled in management development programs.

The men were able to accommodate to less than optimal work gratification. "After all," they would say, "more than 50 percent of this is bullshit!" The men chose success—personal success, not success for the corporation—and were both pleased and surprised when the two meshed.

The women chose work gratification and, in doing so, relinquished their control over their expressed need for success in the corporation—and were hurt and confused when they received neither.

Fortunately Georgia sought clarification of her confusion. She confronted her superior regarding the ratings that she received. A rating session placed her sixth out of twenty-one managers. She felt that her work and her contribution deserved a higher rating and sought clarification.

Georgia: "I asked my boss if it was my ability, if it was the time and energy that I put into the job, if I needed more experience, or if it was image management. He said—quite frankly—'If you didn't have a family, I think you would be ranked as number two or three.'

"In this company a family exists to support your career.

I have given up a lot of power that I could have at work because of my family responsibilities. I can't go out and have a drink after work because I have to pick up my son. This makes me lose my spot in the political network. I can't always stay late, even another fifteen minutes or a half hour. This makes me look like I'm not committed to the work effort. I don't feel free to travel every week, and here again, it makes me look like I'm not committed to the work effort. The whole problem with respect to my ratings is one of image, not expertise. There has to be a way of handling the image problem."

There is a way of handling the image problem. But first, let's review the total pattern of Georgia's behaviors that caused her to lose both her control over her work and her discretionary authority:

- First, she demonstrated poor image management.
- Second, she did not respond to the requests that came into her department on a selective basis.
- Third, she adopted a nice-guy image.
- Fourth, she used courtesy as a rationalization for not aggressively pursuing her business needs.
- Fifth, she chose as her mission goals that were antithetical to those that would make her successful in her organization.
- Sixth, she settled for nonnegotiable rewards.

In order to be able to modify Georgia's behaviors so that she can achieve the level of success that she wants and in order for her to have more discretionary authority over her work situation, it is necessary to see how each of the behaviors are related to each other.

The threefold combination of *nice-guy image, nonassertiveness,* and *poor image management* can be corrected by packaging the nice actions so that they are viewed as valuable to the company, recognizing the difference between corporate behavior and personal behavior, and verbalizing, if not practicing, the image that is considered successful in the company.

Packaging Nice-Guy Actions

In Georgia's case, her nice-guy actions led her to assume responsibility for a number of little projects. No needs assesssment had been done that justified the amount of time she spent on them, and the projects she had been assigned suffered as a result.

Packaging is what gets the customer to buy, and in this case the customer is the boss. A needs assessment can be performed after the fact and a number of little projects can be found to have a common denominator if you look hard enough. Bond paper, typeset copy, glossy covers, and company colors are all packaging techniques that are used for external clients and customers. Use them for internal clients and customers as well. This may all be facade, gingerbread, icing; call it what you like, but when you recognize that it is these efforts that allow you to meet the needs you have recognized for the company and get you the support you need from your superiors as well, it becomes more than just icing—it becomes a technique that you can use to increase your discretionary authority.

These techniques may be hard for the purist to accept, but they are not difficult to implement.

Am I saying that the ends justify the means? Most definitely!

Corporate versus Personal Behavior

I'll never forget the day when I was giving a workshop to a group of high-powered managers and was walking down an aisle of the seminar room and spied an untied shoelace—and almost bent down to tie it. At the time my own children were in grade school, and my behavior as a mother was spilling over to the work place. I was also consulting for several companies and assisting them in drawing up affirmative action programs as well as conducting seminars to effect behavior change in white males and their treatment of women and blacks within corporate structures. I invariably had heated discussions that led to some very heavy arguments after the seminars with the man I was dating at the time. Those arguments were the result of my behavior at work spilling over into my love life. This is far different from the pattern that men have been accused of: bringing home their work problems and concerns.

It is not the work issues that interfere with home and parenting, but behaviors from home and parenting that interfere with the portrayal of businesslike and business needs behavior.

Here are the major contrasts between the abdicator at work and the working bitch:

- The abdicator at work is fearful of offending; the working bitch takes the offensive.
- The abdicator at work presents work information using the "I" message; the working bitch saves the "I" message for her personal interactions.
- The abdicator at work says, "I can't be that way"; the working bitch pretends to be that way whether she is or not.
- The abdicator at work cajoles her subordinates and plays the coquette with her superior; the working bitch makes appropriate business demands and stands her ground and speaks her piece.
- The abdicator at work is inappropriately courteous; the working bitch courts power.
- The abdicator at work is open in her discussions, disregarding business realities; the working bitch tempers her honesty, maintaining a professional image within business restraints.

- The abdicator at work avoids confronting criticism; the working bitch invites feedback.
- The abdicator at work allows her ego to interfere with her work activities; the working bitch acts in spite of damaged ego.
- The abdicator at work personalizes work situations; the working bitch keeps them within business parameters and approaches them objectively.
- The abdicator at work settles for negotiable rewards; the working bitch pragmatically identifies her success criteria and takes action to meet them.

Just as in love relationships and in parenting, behaviors that allow us to abdicate in work situations cannot be modified on a hit-and-miss basis. Behaviors have to be viewed as patterns or pathways where the end result of these patterns is clearly identified. Only then are we able to understand the impact of each of the behaviors and then implement modification techniques and methods that will interfere with them.

Chapter Eighteen

The Three-Step Process Toward Authority

The following diagram outlines the abdicator's pathway to compliance from personalizing the corporate environment to the ultimate result of abdicator behaviors in the work place—the settling for nonnegotiable rewards. Continue reading the table and discussion on the three-step process that follow the diagram. Consider the reading as homework. Then practice the interference techniques outlined and discussed in this chapter.

DIAGRAM 3. The Abdicator's Pathway to Compliance

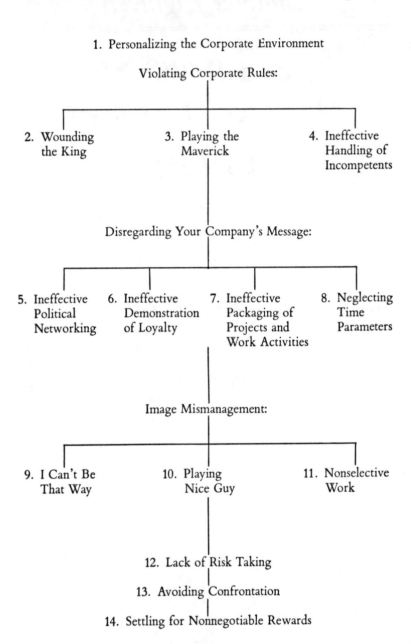

1. Personalizing the Corporate Environment

Violating Corporate Rules:

2. Wounding the King   3. Playing the Maverick   4. Ineffective Handling of Incompetents

Disregarding Your Company's Message:

5. Ineffective Political Networking   6. Ineffective Demonstration of Loyalty   7. Ineffective Packaging of Projects and Work Activities   8. Neglecting Time Parameters

Image Mismanagement:

9. I Can't Be That Way   10. Playing Nice Guy   11. Nonselective Work

12. Lack of Risk Taking

13. Avoiding Confrontation

14. Settling for Nonnegotiable Rewards

The Three-Step Process Toward Authority

The following section outlines the *Three-Step Process Toward Authority* and allows the reader to see at a glance the abdicating behaviors, their impact, and the interference techniques used to offset them.

Here again, as in the Three-Step Process Toward Equality in love relationships, and the Three-Step Process Toward Strength in parenting, the implementation of the techniques that run interference with settling for less than what you want and less than you are capable of in work situations requires only practice. No complex or highly technical training is necessary to effect changes in behaviors that we use to handle daily interactions. Recognizing the behavior and understanding its impact and the benefits that you will receive from changing that behavior are all you need to begin immediately to move from compliance to authority in work situations.

TABLE 3. THE THREE-STEP PROCESS TOWARD AUTHORITY

Step I: Recognizing Abdicating Behavior	Step II: Understanding the Impact	Step III: Practicing Interference Techniques
1. Personalizing the corporate environment	Oversensitivity to inequalities Lowers self-confidence Limits ability to problem-solve and challenge violations	• Learn formal and informal policies and procedures • Review sex ratios and compare your company to industry-wide figures • Determine front-line positions and departments
2. Violating corporate rules: wounding the king	Generates hostility Destroys ability to develop discretionary authority	• Don't challenge overtly • Give boss credit • Monitor your ego needs • Make use of your political network
3. Violating corporate rules: playing the maverick	General mistrust Generates hostility from peers and intimidates subordinates	• Remain within a reasonable range of prestated deadlines • Put work efforts in company jargon • Seriously consider changing jobs if there is a significant distance between your work style and ambition and your company's
4. Violating corporate rules: ineffective handling of incompetents	Perceived as lacking leadership, managerial, and development skills	• Avoid when possible • Explain task in small doses • Train, don't develop

Step I: Recognizing Abdicating Behavior	Step II: Understanding the Impact	Step III: Practicing Interference Techniques
5. Disregarding your company's message: ineffective politcial networking	Loss of information Loss of support Viewed as non-team player	• Check out trends, objectives, and rumors • Incorporate the language in your conversation, memos, and reports • Set aside one hour per day for political networking • Seek out politically reliable people
6. Disregarding your company's message: ineffective demonstration of loyalty	Reduction of support Damages political networking Viewed as non-team player Generates hostility	• Keep negative comments to yourself • Actively support superior and department • Keep away from shit disturbers • If the situation seriously violates your principles, change jobs
7. Disregarding your company's message: ineffective packaging of projects and work activities	Causes difficulty in selling projects Offsets work efforts Causes frustration and makes work tiresome	• Spend between 10% and 25% of the total time to complete the project on packaging • Use one-on-one and group selling techniques • Listen and respond to both positive and negative comments
8. Disregarding your company's message: neglecting time parameters	Perceived as a lack of commitment to company and to career	• Plan evening work on a regular basis • Maintain visibility during overtime hours • Keep family talk to a minimum

Step I: Recognizing Abdicating Behavior	Step II: Understanding the Impact	Step III: Practicing Interference Techniques
9. Image mismanagement: I can't be that way	Inhibits behavioral growth	• Objectify your language pattern • Actively seek tangible benefits from your superior • Delegate low-priority work to subordinates • Understand compensation, benefits, and perks of your position
10. Image mismanagement: playing nice guy	Aids process of settling for non-negotiable rewards Reduces perceived dominance Positions you to be taken advantage of	• Actively practice business role • List required support, information, and assistance • Actively seek requirements from business associates
11. Image mismanagement: nonselective work	Fosters low visibility Devalues your work efforts Allows you to be taken advantage of Positions you to settle for non-negotiable rewards	• Package tasks for high visibility • Delegate low-visibility requests for work • Assess all requests for the benefits you will receive

Step I: Recognizing Abdicating Behavior	Step II: Understanding the Impact	Step III: Practicing Interference Techniques
12. Lack of risk taking	Limits discretionary authority Prevents the recognition of alternatives and options Positions for acceptance of nonnegotiable rewards	• Prepare financially for risk taking • Keep résumé updated • Maintain relationships with professional recruiters • Choose small risks and slowly graduate to the larger ones
13. Avoiding confrontation	Loss of information Loss of potential to solve problems Positions you to settle for nonnegotiable rewards	• Actively listen to all feedback • Invite recommendations for improvement • Pick your time for the confrontation • Set up your ego to accept criticism and challenge
14. Settling for nonnegotiable rewards	Squanders time better used in career building Causes "Job is a dead space syndrome" Causes frustration and discontent that invades other areas	• Initiate a needs-and-wants work ledger • Place your needs in order of priority • Use the techniques to satisfy needs not being met that are suggested for risk taking and confrontation

1. Recognizing Abdicating Behavior: Personalizing the corporate environment

Personalizing the corporate environment by believing that you have been singled out for special negative treatment, such as the withholding of perks or the unequal distribution of benefits and compensation, excessive demands regarding either time or productivity, withholding of respect of position, or the withholding of authority that you believe is required to carry out the task.

Understanding the Impact

Personalizing the corporate environment is reflected in an oversensitivity to inequalities and generally limits the individual from being able to determine solutions or challenge rights that have been violated.

In addition, it generates the "I must be doing something wrong" attitude and erodes self-confidence, leading to frustration, poor morale, and lowered productivity.

Practicing Interference Techniques

- Learn and study the formal policies, rules, and regulations of your company.
- Seek clarification of anything that you do not understand from personnel and from co-workers.
- Learn the informal rules and procedures of your company.
- Learn what positions and what departments are considered to be at the front lines of the total operation. Understanding this aspect can show you how to begin to position yourself to be in the groups accorded respect and deserving of equal benefits.
- Review sex ratios within all positional levels in your organization and compare them with industry-wide figures.

2. Recognizing Abdicating Behavior: Violating corporate rules: Wounding the king

Directly challenging your immediate superior regardless of the value of correctness of the challenge. Taking over at meetings, suggesting more efficient procedures, and attempting to influence policy of the department and leaving no doubt as to whose idea it is. Whereas the ineffective demonstration of loyalty is a corporate sin by omission, wounding the king is an active and overt violation of the corporate rule that will without doubt set up insurmountable obstacles to your success goal regardless of the class that you choose.

Understanding the Impact

This behavior generates hostility from your superiors and removes support for you and your work activities. It makes you an undesirable within the corporate team. This behavior destroys the ability to develop discretionary authority over your work activities. Even a successful attempt, one that kills the king, will make you less attractive to the power brokers. Their only thought will be, "When is it my turn?"

Practicing Interference Techniques

- Never challenge the boss overtly, either in a group or in a one-on-one discussion.
- Flatter, don't flatten.
- Give him/her credit for the ideas that you come up with. Eventually your input will be recognized as you use well-placed comments in your political network.
- While it is not necessary to keep your smarts entirely to yourself, it is necessary that you refrain from being the smart ass, the intellectual, the logician, especially if these last two qualities are not known qualities of your superior.

3. Recognizing Abdicating Behavior: Violating corporate rules: Playing the maverick

Accomplishing the task or project in unorthodox fashion or completing it far in advance of the deadline that was determined as appropriate by superiors or peers. Expecting subordinates to put forth effort equal to your own.

Understanding the Impact

Mistrust is the impact for any employees whose lack of convention and unorthodox methods become recognized. In addition, rate breaking can generate hostility from superiors and peers who may not be as capable as you are; it engenders fear and intimidates subordinates.

Mistrust, hostility, and intimidation from these three levels damages your ability to develop political networks, causes you to suffer the informal methods of punishment, and sets you up to receive nonnegotiable rewards.

Practicing Interference Techniques

- Stay within a reasonable range of prestated deadlines, decreasing time to complete projects and work by no more than 10 percent. The 10 percent will give you the look of a comer. Anything beyond that will make you suspect.
- Put work efforts in the company jargon. This helps to reduce the maverick tone to your work.
- If your ambition time line, promotions, and increased job responsibility are geared to a faster climb than is expected in your company, seriously consider changing jobs.

4. Recognizing Abdicating Behavior: Violating corporate rules: Ineffective handling of incompetents

The inability to interact with individuals whose skills and expertise are mediocre or incompetent.

Understanding the Impact
The inability to work effectively with any level of expertise or talent is viewed as an inability to take leadership roles, an inability to manage or supervise, and an inability to train or develop.

Practicing Interference Techniques
- Whenever possible, avoid a working relationship with individuals you determine to be less competent than you are. Their lesser abilities, lack of conceptual skills, and the difficulty with which incompetents implement work activities add another level of frustration to the work place.
- If unavoidable, use explanations that break up the task as much as possible. The farther the incompetents are from your level of expertise, the less able they will be to understand the total picture, causing irritation for them as well as for you.
- The key here is *to train, not develop*. To train is to teach the task at hand. To develop is to guide the individual to go beyond his or her demonstrated potential.
- Do not play nice guy here or use inappropriate courtesy because you feel sorry for them. These actions will hinder your primary goal and success criteria regardless of the class that you chose for yourself.

5. Recognizing Abdicating Behavior: Disregarding your company's message: Ineffective political networking
Failing to focus on political networking. Political networking is sensitivity to present and changing organizational trends and the active participation of utilizing those trends to meet the goals of your personal success criteria. The abdicator who is ineffective at political networking does not focus on organizational trends. Her lack of focus may be the result of studied neglect—"I don't have to pay attention to those things. My work

speaks for itself." Or her lack of focus may be the result of a negative connotation that she attaches to the use of corporate politics—"I don't like to play politics. It's dishonest."

Understanding the Impact

Whether through ignorance or with awareness, the woman who is ineffective at political networking suffers the same results. She loses information and support, and she is perceived both as naive and as a nonteam player.

A second impact is terminal positioning, whether her success goal is advancement or increased discretionary authority and more freedom over work assignments. Whereas it might not overtly affect you in your present position, it can impede your movement up the corporate ladder.

Effective political networking is not as important for those women who choose class one success—those who wish to remain in their present classifications and maintain low- to middle-management positions. (Review classifications discussed in Chapter 14.) It becomes increasingly important as you change your success criteria and move from class two—desiring upward mobility— to class four—wanting more discretionary authority and increased freedom over task assignment.

For women with class three success goals—for those women who desire upward mobility and are recognized experts in their field—ineffective political networking causes them to be typecast and prevents them from moving into other areas.

Practicing Interference Techniques

- Read the company's objectives and long-term planning proposals. Study them, and make sure you understand the concepts and the buzz words.
- Pay attention to rumors, and check out their source as best you can.

- Make a point to get out of your office and seek out those individuals who are considered politically astute and reliable. It only takes a few minutes of conversation to pick up information about what's going on.
- Stay clear of those with poor reputations. Birds who flock together are considered to come from the same nest, whether they do or not.
- Check out trends and rumors both within your department and external to it.
- Do your best to understand how your department will be affected and how and where you can impact trends within it.
- Find out what current work is being touted by the power brokers in your company. People who are conversant with current fads are given more respect and are considered more knowledgeable than those who are not.
- Use new trends, buzz words, and the language of important objectives and long-term goals in your conversation, your memos, and your reports.
- Take at least one hour per day to further your political networking.
- Put this list of interference techniques on your personal calendar and *don't fall behind*. You can't catch up on trends and information that has passed you by.

6. Recognizing Abdicating Behavior: Disregarding your company's message: Ineffective demonstration of loyalty

Failing to demonstrate active participation and support of ideas and activities of the individual's immediate superior. Support of activities outside of the individual's specific department and support of the company as a whole run second and third, respectively, to that shown to the immediate superior. Ineffective demonstration of loyalty is displayed by the support of ideas or activities without regard to their origins, and which may be either different from or counter to any work, project, or activity that is the charge of your specific department. Ineffective loyalty is most often displayed by women who create the nice-guy image and who engage in nonselective work.

Understanding the Impact

The primary impact of an ineffective demonstration of loyalty is the reduction of support and damage to the individual's political networking. In addition, the behavior generates hostility where there is a direct conflict between the immediate superior's actions and the actions of individuals outside of the department—regardless of the relative benefits these actions have for the good of the company.

If coupled with the nice-guy image, the woman is seen as naive at best. Barring the nice-guy image, she is seen as a nonteam player, a shit disturber, and one not to be trusted. In both cases, she positions herself to be the recipient of nonnegotiable rewards. The more aggressive she is in the championing of the right causes for the wrong people, the more hostility she generates.

Practicing Interference Techniques

- Keep negative comments to yourself.
- If the issue is too glaring for you to withhold comment on, use objective language in your discussions and keep to the facts.
- In the presentation of facts, keep in mind that within the corporate structure tempered honesty is the better route to power.
- Actively and overtly support the concepts, projects, activities, and ideas of your immediate superior and the person in charge of your department.
- Once again, this requires a reevaluation of your daily work calendar so that you can book in the time to demonstrate your support.
- Spend, at the minimum, three separate fifteen-minute

time periods per week verbalizing your support to individuals whom you know will get the message back to your superior.

- Keep away from shit disturbers as much as possible.
- If the situation becomes one that is at odds with a principle you do not feel you can violate, think seriously about changing jobs and use the interference technique suggested for the lack of risk taking.

7. Recognizing Abdicating Behavior: Disregarding your company's message: Ineffective packaging of projects and work activities

Focusing energies only on the content of the work and relinquishing control over how the work will be received. Packaging work projects and activities involves interpersonal and group selling skills and the use of appropriate materials, format, and written language. It is a combination of proper image management and appropriate work presentation. The abdicator who is ineffective at packaging focuses her energies only on the content of the work or project and relinquishes the control she could take over how the work is received. She does this by neglecting both interpersonal and group selling and materials presentation.

Understanding the Impact

One of the primary impacts of ineffective packaging is the difficulty that results in selling the project. When you have expended effort in the conceptualization and implementation of any work, not selling it and not having your effort appreciated only lead to frustration.

Routinized work activities require as much packaging as special projects. The lack of appreciation and the resulting frustration have a direct effect on the energy and enthusiasm that are demonstrated on the job. It then becomes a vicious cycle, and the employee's neglect of packaging and presentation is viewed with increasing disfavor as her frustration becomes more and more noticeable. Work efforts that have been expended are offset, and less and less gratification is forthcoming. The work and the job become unpleasant. In the absence of pleasure and energy, the job becomes more tiring than warranted.

The negative results are not limited to the single project in question but usually follow the individual from project to project and involve all work activities. At their worst, poor packaging techniques generate a "here she comes again" attitude among her co-workers and superiors. Subordinates pick up on the lack of energy and enthusiasm and deliver low productivity and poorer quality of work results.

Practicing Interference Techniques

- Spend between 10 and 25 percent of the total time it takes you to complete a work activity or a project on packaging. We are talking about *your success* here, not the company's. Though it might be true that you could accomplish more for the company if you sit in your office and neglect the interpersonal and group selling skills and resist going to an outside printer or resist insisting on special type from your secretary, thus increasing the time she will have to spend on the project's clerical preparation, it is also true that you will be relinquishing the chance to take an opportunity to further your own success goals.
- Make people remember *how well the project went over, how many people you got on the bandwagon,* and *how well it was presented.*
- Show energy and enthusiasm. Interpersonal and group selling techniques require a behavioral display of energy and enthusiasm.
- As soon as you begin a project, take fifteen minutes out of your day and actively seek out people to tell them about the project. Be sure to use the buzz words that you've picked up from your political networking.
- Pay close attention to the responses that you hear.

- Quote the positive responses, especially if they come from one of the power brokers.
- Get back to the negative responses. Usually a phone call will do. Thank the person for his/her input and tell him/her how you have incorporated it into a project.
- Change a detractor into a supporter by following diligently the previous step..
- Use one-on-one selling. It is usually easier than group selling.
- Find a benefit in the project that will turn on the person you are selling to. That's a key to one-on-one selling.
- Remember, one of the benefits you are offering is that you now become part of their political network.
- The second part of effective packaging is materials presentation. There should be no need to explain that *neatness counts*. You need to take the concept a bit further, however. Pay attention to format; type of print; high-quality paper; glossy covers with a catchy slogan if the project warrants it, and even if it doesn't.
- Spend additional dollars and time, even if there has been a drive to reduce paper costs and increase productivity. If you don't, you're being penny wise and pound foolish with your career.
- Always keep in mind that it's your success we want to enhance here, not the company's, and the two are definitely not always mutually compatible.
- Seek out the last successful project that earned its designer heavy points from the power brokers in the company and follow a monkey-see monkey-do approach.
- If you're not sure how he or she did the last successful project, ask about it. The asking will aid you in two ways. It will give you information on how it's done, and it will gain you another member for your political network. Most people like to feel that they have skills to teach you; by asking, you ingratiate them.

8. Recognizing Abdicating Behavior: Disregarding your company's message: Neglecting time parameters

Behaving as though your job were a five-day, nine-to-five interruption in your life by spending no more than the formally stated time requirements on the job.

Understanding the Impact

The woman who spends only the minimum time required on the job, regardless of the success criteria she has chosen, is perceived as lacking commitment to the company and is considered to be a worker and not a serious careerist, regardless of the quality of the work she produces. The majority of corporate organizations view input, not output.

Rather than being valued for her ability, the woman who can work twice as fast and therefore half as long is perceived as not being part of the committed hard-working company team.

Practicing Interference Techniques

- Remain after regular closing time a minimum of four evenings per month, whether you have work to do or not.
- Scatter the pattern of these evenings, choosing different days and some weeks remaining two evenings and skipping a week.
- Make sure that you are visible by mentioning that you will be staying late to finish up some work or handle some routine paperwork that you want to catch up on.
- Show up at least one Saturday per month and again make sure that you do it with visibility.
- Keep family talk to a minimum, especially discussions about the drain on your time that your role as mother and housekeeper demands.
- When small talk involves that issue, speak in glowing

terms of the support for your career and your work that you have at home—whether you have it or not—and do your best to insure that the power brokers hear about it.

9. Recognizing Abdicating Behavior: Image mismanagement: I can't be that way

Refusing to portray behaviors that bear negative connotations when applied to women, such as nonfeminine, overly pushy, aggressive, calculating, too businesslike, and bitchy.

Understanding the Impact

The primary impact of the "I can't be that way" behavior is to inhibit both the recognition and the behaviors that are required by the corporate success structure. In addition, the refusal to adapt to required corporate behavior patterns typecasts the abdicator and begins the process of causing her to settle for nonnegotiable rewards.

Practicing Interference Techniques

- Use language that will counter the "I can't be that way" approach.
- Remove as many personal pronouns as you can from your language pattern.
- Objectifying your language pattern will benefit you in two ways: First, it stops you from giving personal input where objective input is required; Second, it gives you the appearance of being in control of the situation, whether you are or not.
- Remove weak modifiers from your language pattern—"somewhat," "little," "perhaps." These modifiers sugarcoat, soften, and detract from an image of strength and authority. Interfere with the "I can't be that way" approach by taking specific actions with superiors and subordinates and by understanding and actively seeking all the benefits of your position.

Action with Superior:

- Choose something that you want from your superior that will result in a tangible benefit to you: a project or task force that you want to work on that will increase your visibility; an outside or internal training seminar that you want to attend.
- List the benefits you will gain if he/she grants your request and those that he/she or the department will gain.
- Choose the timing for your request carefully. Mondays are usually bad days. It's the beginning of the week and he/she is probably back from the short weekend respite full of renewed vigor. Whether the energy is real or imagined, your boss thinks it's real. It doesn't do you any good to interfere with it.
- Use Thursdays for requests. Thursdays are good days in most companies. Plans, projects, and committees that met on Mondays are becoming routine. Everyone is taking a breather, and the time is better for requests.
- Don't surprise your superior with the request. Set him/her up for it by announcing on Tuesday that you need some time, help, advice.
- Pick the buzz word that you think turns the boss on.
- In outward appearance, what you present is a request. From your perspective, view the request as a demand.
- Listen carefully to any objections your superior might have and answer them with the benefits that you have listed for him.
- Keep an understanding of your own benefits to yourself.
- The combination of making a request and having it granted begin to set you up as an individual both capable and deserving of increased responsibility and authority: in both his/her mind and yours. It begins to break the pattern of settling for nonnegotiable rewards.

Action with Subordinates:

- Review your present work activities and place them

on a list in decreasing order of importance both to the success of your overall job responsibilities and in decreasing order of visibility.
- Check off the last two activities, and begin the process of delegating them to subordinates.
- Offer the work to them as a benefit, but be careful not to promise anything you can't deliver. That will only destroy your credibility. This helps to free you for more success-oriented actions and enhances your reputation as an able supervisor

Position Benefits:
- Review the compensation, benefits, and perks that by policy are granted to people in your position. Compensation in the form of salary is not equally distributed among similar positions by most companies. The greatest inequity is the continuing sex discrimination in this area. In addition, it is against the law not to have salary disclosure.
- Although there is an unwritten rule that salary is not to be discussed, use careful questioning and probing to determine where you stand.
- If you discover an inequity, confront your superior with it.
- Perks of the position are as important as compensation and benefits, not for the present state of your bank balance but for its future endowment.
- Office furniture, clerical help, windows, and carpeting are all part of the image that either adds to or detracts from the degree of authority and influence that you can exercise.
- Playing nice guy or behaving with a courtesy that belongs in your personal and not your business life withholds both the perks and the authority.

10. Recognizing Behavior: Image mismanagement: Playing nice guy
Assuming secondary role of helper/protector in business environment; sugarcoating or softening requests for in-

formation or support you require to accomplish the task; acquiescing and relinquishing role of equal or superior in business environment.

Understanding the Impact
This behavior aids the process of settling for nonnegotiable rewards. It reduces perceived dominance and hinders the role of manager or supervisor. This behavior positions you to be taken advantage of and helps to create the image of woman as opposed to worker.

Practicing Interference Techniques
● Choose one individual per month and practice your actual business role.
● List areas of support, information, and assistance that you require in order to accomplish routine tasks associated with your position.
● Set aside a given time every week and have as your action plan the gathering of support, information, and assistance from the individual you have chosen.
● Begin in your own department. It is helpful here to start with a subordinate over whom you have authority by virtue of your position.
● Follow through the second month with a peer, and the third month with your superior.
● Do not attempt to practice this new behavior with all three levels at once.
● Use a slow and deliberate posture for change. This will allow you to monitor the behavior, making corrections as you practice it. Behavior changes that occur too swiftly are seen as aberrant.

11. Recognizing Abdicating Behavior: Nonselective work
Responding to all requests for work and help without thought to the benefits you will accrue from your involvement in them and without setting them into

priority according to their origination or your previously designated work objectives.

Understanding the Impact

Responding to requests on a nonselective basis can result in a perception of your reduced value to the company—"If she has time for all that, what can her job really contribute?" Nonselective work can foster low visibility, especially if you are responding to requests that come from individuals who have little influence and are far removed from the power brokers.

In addition to lowered perceived value and low visibility, you place yourself in the position to be taken advantage of and add to the process of settling for nonnegotiable rewards.

Practicing Interference Techniques

- Package those tasks that you have a need to do by virtue of the work gratification they will afford you so that they will receive high visibility.
- Keep in mind that work gratification and achieving your success criteria do not go hand in hand. Remember that you are there to help yourself, not to play helper.
- Evaluate all requests according to the information that you have gleaned from your political networking.
- Delegate oft-repeated and low-visibility requests to subordinates or suggest peers that can handle them.
- Develop a system that will allow you to assess requests according to the tangible benefits you will receive if you meet them.

12. Recognizing Abdicating Behavior: Lack of risk taking

Failing to speak up for oneself and focusing on security needs. Most often expressed as an inability to speak up for oneself, lack of risk taking is in that respect similar to avoiding confrontation. Lack of risk taking is also displayed through a focus on the security needs to keep a position, even if it does not lead to the accomplishment of your chosen success criteria. Lack of risk taking is, therefore, a combination of not risking confrontation and not risking change.

Understanding the Impact
Avoiding risks leads to the limiting of discretionary authority over work activities. In addition, the process of opting not to risk prevents the individual from recognizing alternatives and options in both present and future positions and careers and helps to position them for accepting nonnegotiable rewards.

Recognizing Interference Techniques
- Prepare yourself as soon as possible financially. A comfortable bank balance helps to keep the balance between satisfying your success criteria and complying with company directives tipped on your side of the scale.
- Whether you want to or not and regardless of how satisfied you are with your present position and company, update your résumé every six months and be aware of openings in positions in other companies.
- Keep an ongoing relationship with at least three major professional recruiters in your field of expertise.
- The primary reward, and the most tangible one that will attest to your success, is the amount of compensation that you receive.
- Actively seek a compensation increase of 30 percent every eighteen months.

13. Recognizing Abdicating Behavior: Avoiding confrontation
The inability to challenge affronts, such as lack of equality of compensation, perks, and benefits. Rejecting criti-

cism by refusing to invite feedback to clarify it and learn from it.

Understanding the Impact
Avoiding confrontation results in the loss of information and the loss of potential ability to solve problems. In addition, it leads you again closer to accepting nonnegotiable rewards.

Practicing Interference Techniques
- Keep your receiving antennae on high during all feedback on your work.
- If the evaluation is less than you think you should have received, ask for methods that could have improved it.
- Listen to peers and subordinates as well as to superiors. Improvement comes from all sources, and everyone is flattered by your active listening to what they have to say. Again, this can increase your political network.
- Keep your language in the objective realm, removing as much as possible the personal pronouns in your discussions.
- Pick your time for the confrontation. Say, "I want your feedback on this; when can we get together on it? Now isn't a good time, I have to wrap up the widget report."
- Picking your time allows you to prepare for the confrontation.
- Your work is going to be challenged; prepare not only the content response but your ego as well.
- Five minutes before you go into the confrontation think about the last time you made love, the love your children have for you, how great you looked last Saturday night, and the positive balance in your checkbook.
- While you need to take into account the job market,

geographical changes, family concerns, the life-style in your present location, and the life-style that your current work activity provides you with, you do not need to focus on "How will it look if I change jobs too often," if those changes result in 30 percent or more increases in compensation. "Changing jobs too often" is a boardroom story told by corporate personnel managers and has no bearing in the real world of work.

- Remember this rule: competence begets compensation.
- Carefully choose the battleground for your risk taking.
- The important criteria to recognize here is that winning counts and losing discounts.
- Choose small battles first that you can win, and use those wins to gain you a reputation. The more small ones you win, the more able you are to win the larger ones by default, and the more comfortable you will feel in the combat zone.

14. Recognizing Abdicating Behavior: Settling for nonnegotiable rewards

Following the pathway to compliance (see diagram 3, in this chapter). While the abdicator at work positions herself for nonnegotiable rewards through the expression of many of the behaviors within the pathway to compliance, settling for them represents that final point that many working women find themselves in where the job becomes less a career and more a space of time that must be endured between those other activities with which she fills her life. It is at this point that few efforts to break away are made and where a nine-to-five mentality takes hold. The process is a slow one, and to a large extent, it is not recognized primarily because it has grown through a lack of change and a maintenance of sameness.

Understanding the Impact

Given the slow progression of settling for nonnegotiable rewards, its primary impact is the squandering of time that could have been used to build a career with its rightful compensation and benefits. In addition, time has been lost that could have been better utilized to create a life situation within the work place and that would foster growth and generate excitement.

The "job is a dead space" syndrome because of the large percentage of time spent on the job eventually invades other areas of life activities where they too lose their color and zest. Such a milieu causes the individual to be both less interested in the world around her and less interesting to it.

Practicing Interference Techniques

Interfering with a habitual process of settling for non-negotiable rewards will take time and honesty. It requires that on a regular basis you take the time out of an area of your life and prepare a needs-and-wants ledger similar to the one you prepared in understanding your love relationship—and in parenting—but this time the content is work.

Phase I
- Take out your work calendar and whether you choose personal days, vacation days, or sick days ink in at least four days over a period of the next two months to work on your needs-and-wants ledger.

- You can't do this as homework at night. You already have activities that take up your time, and trying to eke it out of prearranged obligations, responsibilities, or leisure time is both insufficient and could strain your other relationships and cause you to abdicate the satisfaction of your needs in those areas.

- The needs-and-wants work ledger begins the process of helping you to make a life—not just a living—out of your work activities.

Phase II
- Once you have determined the days that you will spend on your needs-and-wants ledger, choose an atmosphere where you can be free of other concerns to work on it.

- It is difficult to begin your ledger at home. There are usually distractions whether or not the kids are in school or your husband is at work. There is laundry to do, a room that needs attention, a closet that you have been wanting to reorganize. These represent distractions, and few of us are able to resist the temptation that they cause.

- In addition to the distractions, your home base, because of its familiarity, is not the best place to consider change.

- Changing your environment while you are working on your ledger helps to set you up for change and helps to keep your focus on the task.

Phase III
- Begin your needs-and-wants ledger by making a list of what you want from your work life.

- A good starting point: determine what class of success criteria you want. At this point, fantasize freely. What is utopia in the work place for you?

- Include such items as compensation, benefits, freedom to choose tasks, sense of accomplishment, work gratification, team work and support, reinforcement and recognition, achievement, growth, geographical location, and the use of abilities, expertise, and intellect.

Phase IV
- List your needs in order of priority.
- Make sure these are your own priorities, not those that you think you should have or someone else's priorities.

Phase V
- Now begin to check off those needs that are being satisfied in your present situation and those that you are not receiving.
- Look within your present situation for areas within which to satisfy the needs that you have not been receiving. Use the techniques suggested for lack of risk taking and avoiding confrontation to help you get them satisfied.
- Remember that as you satisfy one need, others will surface, and they too will require work as you go about the process of fulfilling them.

As you go through this process you may recognize the need to change jobs, change careers, or take some time out of the work place to investigate other areas. The five-phase process of developing a needs-and-wants work ledger allows you to understand your needs and to develop the skills to have them satisfied, and helps you to take the necessary actions to fulfill them. It provides you with the choice between making a living or making a life.

Chapter Nineteen

The Working Bitch

You want to know how I became successful. Two ways. I looked for my next promotion from the day I got the job, and if I didn't have the authority to get the job done and they wouldn't give it to me, I quit and found a company that would. Any woman who tells you that she couldn't quit or couldn't get a job that gave her the authority to do what they hired her for is talking bullshit.

Separating out the bullshit was the euphemism that Regina used to describe using rationalizations, the boss, the company, or your ignorance as an excuse for not getting where you want to be in your career. Regina's approach to success within the corporate structure has earned her a career that started fifteen years ago and today places her in a class of less than 2 percent of all working women. As director of corporate communications handling all advertising, public relations, and promotion for the high-tech side of a Fortune 500 firm, Regina commands a salary of $80,000 and enjoys a healthy package of stock options, pension benefits, and insurance protection.

Her three-pronged approach to career advancement requires the following: first, that the company share equally in the responsibility for her success; second, that she maintain a consistent and well-guarded focus on her next promotion; and third, that she show no hesitation in risking job change in order to achieve her goals.

Unlike the abdicator, Regina did not avoid risk taking. And further, with well-calculated planning she red-flagged the event that would trigger her need to take those risks. If she didn't receive the support she required, she was ready to go where that support was available.

Her success goal was clear and in sight—the next promotion. It was not unrealistic for her to focus on—nor was it an ambiguous mission—helping the company accomplish its objectives. It was a concrete event, the achievement of which was easily identified.

She did not personalize the corporate environment but operated with quid pro quo expectations. She would give her best to the company with the proviso that the company reward her in kind. Her requirement was that the responsibility she took be repaid by the company's obligation to support her efforts and promote her career.

We met for the interview at her office, which bore neither the distinctively sterile look of the stereotypical middle manager nor the cluttered catch-all quality of the overworked and busy-worked first-level manager. There were two or three folders on the desk top, a two-level in and out tray, an ashtray, and a single, apparently fresh, pad of the ever-present white ruled paper. The appearance of the office provided no insight as to the level of her position or her work style. It was not decorated with the "I am climbing the corporate ladder" look that so many of today's managers have affected, nor did it seek to impress or cause concern for the amount of work that might be waiting for its occupant.

In fact, there seemed little about Regina herself that would typecast her as a member of the corporate army's women's division. She wore a short-sleeved burgundy dress and gold jewelry including necklace, earrings and bracelet. Her hair had been tinted a medium blond and cut to just below the ears. She did not display the need to dress the part or to surround herself with the trappings of corporate officialdom in order to insure that she be defined as one of its members.

As we continued the interview, Regina provided more insight into the specifics of how she had managed her career progression.

Regina: "When I started out, I was just grateful to have a job and was really flattered when I was included in work that wasn't already cut out as mine to do. I was certainly doing more work than I was being compensated for, and for the first five years, at least, I fought a lot of battles where I was the only one in the trenches.

"For the first five years I was learning, not just the job and the work, but learning how to get promoted. I learned that you have to think faster and smarter than the people who are at your level, that I had to keep pushing ahead, that I had to be visionary and not reactive. I set out doing the best that I could do and doing what I could do well. Whenever I needed help, I sought counsel from the key guys, the winners. I listened to them, I questioned them, and I gave them my own opinions.

"You just can't lie there and accept everything that comes down the line and follow orders. You need to take broader responsibilities and contribute more than what you've been asked for, but you have to be in an environment that will let you do it."

She also paid her membership dues by initially allowing the balance between the work she delivered and the compensation she received to be tipped in favor of the company. By giving more than was expected of her, she did not follow the abdicator's behavior of by-the-book compliance but instead took every opportunity offered to her to increase her discretionary authority over the tasks she performed.

The key to Regina's success, which clearly separated her from her abdicating sisters, was her focus not only on what she was willing to offer her company—the best that she could do—but on what she required from her company.

The attention she paid to her work and to the success mode that she would portray allowed her to take the mystery out of being permitted to make a living. It also allowed her to join the corporate gameroom as a well-compensated player deserving of respect and authority.

Regina demystified two more myths of corporate life— loyalty and expertise—and pointed out the behaviors that are required for women who wish to counteract them.

Regina: "In the past fifteen years since I started working, I've had five different jobs with five different companies. I always made more on the next job, and I always got more responsibility. When I look for a job I do the interviewing too. You can tell if a company is not going to suit you, and that's a good start. You can't tell if it will be the best for you. You can't until you've worked there, so you can't take a job believing that it is the one that will give you what you want. They haven't proven themselves any more than you have before you start working. You have to set your priorities, and mine were, and still are, to get promoted as fast as I can.

"There's no such thing as knowing the job before you get it and making sure that you can do it before you take it. No one knows that until he or she starts doing the job and really performing in it. Once you know the job you have, you've probably already spent too much time in it and you're certainly ready for the next one. The time to leave a job is when you've almost got it down and before you know what to do in the next step up."

The bottom line of the loyalty myth is that job hopping, particularly when those moves are accompanied by increased compensation and responsibility, does not translate into poor job history. It is a myth that has been promulgated by personnel departments and aided by the cultural demands that women be loyal helpmates, and be sacrificing and uncomplaining.

The myth of expertise is maintained by the secrecy that surrounds many of the informal mechanisms of success—demonstrating proper image management—and is aided by the cultural beliefs that women are less capable than men of performing certain tasks.

Both the personnel policies and the cultural beliefs can be countered by behaviors that permit you to travel the pathway to authority.

Not to practice these behaviors is to permit these policies, demands, and beliefs to affect you on a personal level and to cause you to travel the abdicator's pathway to compliance.

Here is a list of Regina's behaviors:

- Change jobs when you don't get the support you need.
- Play with the winners and avoid the losers.
- Take the next job before you're ready for it.
- Give more than by-the-book compliance.
- Operate with quid pro quo expectations.
- Take well-planned, calculated risks.
- Keep your success goal in clear focus.

These behaviors are aggressive, shrewd, and calculating. Their practice gained Regina success and classify her as a working bitch.

In addition to success, one of the common denominators shared by working bitches is anger and the ability to direct that anger toward constructive actions that would support their success. While unfortunate, it is nevertheless true that the behaviors associated with poor image management are most easily replaced only after a serious and threatening affront to goal realization has been experienced.

Much like experiences in a love union where the woman

who, after years of maintaining a relationship that does not satisfy her needs, is subjected to an event that triggers a conscious awareness of what before was a nagging feeling of discontent and only then is able to take the actions necessary to move toward equality, so also in work situations it is most often after a full-blown affront to her work efforts that the abdicator takes the steps and uses the behaviors that will move her from compliance to authority.

That adversity builds character is certainly not an extraordinary insight. What is insightful is that we can practice those behaviors without undergoing character-building adversity and, further, that having experienced adversity makes you no better at utilizing those behaviors. The adversity simply demonstrates the need for them more dramatically.

It is precisely for this reason that the needs and wants ledger became an important part of our behavioral growth. It allows us to nip the adverse conditions in the bud, to recognize them before they occur and before we aid and abet our detractors and walk willingly to low need satisfaction and the settling for nonnegotiable rewards.

The successful woman must play the role of the working bitch. And as she goes through the process of transforming her behavior from abdicator to bitch, she comes to grips with the fact that her corporate behavior must of necessity be very different from her personal behavior. In this process she gives up sainthood, and the ultimate result is the achievement of success on her terms.

Chapter Twenty

Parallels

The mirror image to the woman as *abdicator* is the man as *accommodator*. And when men behave as accommodators, they present a sadder, more debilitating, and less promising prognosis for the process of moving toward self-determination. The accommodator accepts the status quo of limited loving and superficial nurturing without honest support in his marital and love relationships.

The abdicator practiced denial of these same limits until their frequency and intensity no longer permitted her to hide her discontent.

The accommodator plays the absentee parent without questioning his rights, privileges, and responsibilities as his children become strangers and he adapts to his confusion and despair over his distance from them.

The abdicator relinquished her parenthood and played role reversal with her children until time, age, and social history denied her that hidden place.

The accommodator accepts what he was led to and encouraged himself to believe was a fair and true system of rewards and punishments in the world of work.

The abdicator gave up what she personally experienced and was publicly recognized as an inequitable, disparaging, and discounting career structure.

Accommodation, acceptance, and adaptation make it far more difficult to interfere with habitual behavior patterns than do abdication, active denial, and overt relinquishing of responsibilities. And so the accommodator's path to control, to an enhanced and more encompassing quality of life, is strewn with self-made blocks that are more deeply internalized than are the abdicator's obstacles. It is far more difficult, after all, to fight your own demons than it is to battle your neighbor's.

These observations, coming as they did daily and with every portion of my research from collecting case studies to conducting management and behavioral seminars, did much to, if not soften my personal anger at patriarchy, at least shade it with a budding empathy. That empathy was sorely needed as I observed the contrast between the *true-grit leaders* and the bitches.

The true gritters demand a one-way nurture structure, keep a set of double standards, and insist on the appropriateness of the duplicity that results. The bitches insist on a quid pro quo relationship, abhor the need their partner has to tolerate them, and are explicit about their needs and wants.

The true gritters assume line responsibility for themselves in the realm of parenting and mete out staff support activities to their partners with a largesse that they see as their gender-determined right. The bitches maintain an "I'm the parent here" attitude, eschew outdated labels, and offer all-out protection and unconditional love. The true gritters play a win-lose game in the work place—I win when you lose—and become powerful as they surround themselves with the powerless.

The bitches disavow the "feminine" virtues and build a

power base through hard work and with an ever-cautious eye
on the true gritters.

The behaviors that we witness as these parallels and contrasts become clearer are transformed into actions that confront us and challenge our equality, strength, and authority.

Equality, strength, and authority in love relationships,
parenting, and the work place can only be achieved when
control—or bitch behaviors—replace acquiescing.

Initially the practice of bitch behaviors and the responses
that they generate are disconcerting both for the woman and
the individuals who people her environment. After time and
overt confrontation and communication of needs, wants,
and desires, the behaviors become habitual, the responses
and reactions are accepted in the adult-to-adult realm, and
inequality is replaced by equality, weakness is replaced
by strength, and compliance is replaced by authority. The
adult bitch as a positive self-image supplants the image of
self as a naughty child.

Neither the choices nor changes come without thought
and practice—but we do have the choice after all.

Women who practice abdicating behavior neglect to
transfer the understanding they gain at each stage of their
development between and among the three primary life
spheres.

Women who practice bitch behaviors transfer, test, fine
tune, and integrate their understanding and live more
fulfilling lives.

And if we choose not to change our behaviors, we continue the affront to ourselves as battered wives, we abuse our
children, and we live on the dole that leaves us at the mercy
of whatever is expedient.

None of the abdicators who told their stories here lived the
lives of battered wives—but they all received less than what
they wanted as lovers, as companions, and as caretakers. The
distance between these two conditions of women's reality is
not the distance of extremes, though the content may make it

appear so. It is the distance of the degree to which we permit ourselves to experience pain. And then perhaps the question we must answer is how much pain do I need and how much do I deserve.

The abdicators in parenting did not raise their hands in anger or physically abuse their children, but as mythical mothers they played the role of accessories to child abuse and sought care rather than offered it, as role reversal became the fulcrum upon which their relationships with their children were balanced. Here again, the difference is not in the process but in the content of child abuse. To that end we must ask what our children deserve, what they should be permitted to do, and what they should be allowed to become.

As we watched the abdicator at work, she reflected the courtesy that was miraculously endowed upon her with her femininity, maintained her idealism, and settled for non-negotiable rewards. And we need to answer for ourselves in detail just what rewards we deserve in the world of work.

The voice of feminism in the eighties and beyond needs to be empowered with the intensity that was demonstrated by those who peopled unionism, the suffragette movement, and the initial forays into planned parenthood. Today we are too gentle in our approaches and too circumspect in our behavior. We have become complacent with the gains we have made, and since we are no longer viewed as chattel (though our rights are severely limited in marriage), since we no longer send our children out to early labor (though we withhold from them their just deserts), since we are no longer barred from "masculine" occupations (though we receive 69 cents for every dollar that our lovers receive), we have, given the relative improvement we experienced in the seventies, reduced the intensity of our just claims.

The abdicator's behavior does not give voice to these claims.

We need to become a new breed of heroine. We need to become *bitches*.